Successful Sisters

How To Empower Muslim Women Entrepreneurs in the Modern World

SARAH GULFRAZ

Copyright © 2024 Sarah Gulfraz

Sarah Gulfraz has asserted her right to be identified as the author of this Work in accordance with the Copyright, Designs and Patents Act 1988.

All rights reserved.

No portion of this book may be reproduced in any form, stored in a retrieval system, stored in a database, or published/transmitted in any form or by any means, electronic, mechanical, photocopying, recording or otherwise, without prior written permission of the publisher.

~ **Bismillah** ~

May Allah (swt) accept our efforts and grant us success in this life and the next. Ameen.

In dedication to my loving family and all their support.

Contents

1. Introduction to Muslim Women in Business ... 1
2. Prophet Muhammad as an Entrepreneur ... 21
3. Women Entrepreneurs in Islamic History ... 37
4. Empowering Muslim Women Through Education and Training ... 54
5. Breaking Barriers: Overcoming Challenges in Business ... 72
6. Leadership Development and Skills Enhancement ... 94
7. Future Outlook and Call to Action ... 120
Find Out More ... 142

Chapter One

Introduction to Muslim Women in Business

Overview of Muslim Women's Role in Entrepreneurship

Importance of empowering Muslimah entrepreneurs in the global economy

The landscape of global entrepreneurship is rapidly evolving. It's empowering to see Muslim women stepping up and playing an increasingly significant role in this transformation. Their contributions are not only shaking up traditional business norms but also driving inclusive economic growth like never before.

Recognising the unique challenges and opportunities these incredible women face is important. By empowering Muslimah entrepreneurs, we're not just supporting their individual success but also paving the way for a more equitable and prosperous future for all.

This book explores the empowerment of Muslim women in business, highlighting their contributions, challenges, and opportunities in the modern economy. Each chapter has practical insights, strategies, and resources to help Muslimah entrepreneurs build successful, sustainable businesses.

The Evolving Role of Muslim Women in Entrepreneurship

Muslim women have a rich history of involvement in trade and commerce, dating back to the early days of Islam. Take Khadijah bint Khuwaylid, for example, the first wife of Prophet Muhammad (pbuh), who was a successful businesswoman in her own right. Her role as a trader and her partnership with the Prophet exemplify how pivotal women's roles in economic activities can be. Today, Muslim women are building on this legacy, venturing into various sectors, from technology and finance to fashion and healthcare, breaking stereotypes and challenging societal norms along the way.

Khadijah's example is particularly significant because it underscores the potential for Muslim women to excel in business while staying true to their faith. Her entrepreneurial success and respected status in society illustrate that Islam inherently supports women's economic participation. Modern Muslim women are increasingly looking up to figures like Khadijah, proving that economic empowerment and adherence to faith can go hand in hand.

Empowering Muslim women in entrepreneurship isn't merely a matter of economic necessity – it's also a matter of social justice. The Quran and Hadith are filled with examples and teachings that underscore the importance of women's economic participation. For instance, the Quran states,

> "And do not wish for that by which Allah has made some of you exceed others. For men is a share of what they have earned, and for women is a share of what they have earned. And ask Allah of His bounty. Indeed Allah is ever, of all things, Knowing" (Quran 4:32)

This verse clearly indicates that both men and women are entitled to the fruits of their labour, stressing equality in economic opportunities.

In addition to religious texts, the Hadith literature also includes many instances where women were encouraged to engage in economic activities. For example, Asma bint Abu Bakr. She was a prominent companion of Prophet Muhammad and successfully managed her own business. These precedents set by early Muslim women serve as powerful reminders that women have always had the potential and right to contribute economically.

Importance of Empowering Muslimah Entrepreneurs in the Global Economy

In today's interconnected world, empowering Muslim women entrepreneurs is critical for several reasons:

1. Economic Growth and Development: Women entrepreneurs play a huge role in boosting economic growth and poverty reduction. Studies have shown that women reinvest a substantial portion of their income back into their families and communities. This means better education, healthcare, and community development, creating a ripple effect that benefits society at large. By empowering Muslim women entrepreneurs, we can tap into a vast pool of talent and potential that's traditionally been underutilised. Also, when more women get involved in the economy, it leads to higher GDP growth rates. Equal opportunities for women result in more diverse and robust economic activity. This is especially important in Muslim-majority countries, where economic diversification and innovation are needed to drive sustainable growth.

2. Diversity and Innovation: Diverse leadership teams are not only more innovative but also more effective. Women bring different perspectives and skills to the table, leading to more creative solutions and better business outcomes. Prophet Muhammad (pbuh) said,

> "The seeking of knowledge is obligatory for every Muslim" (Al-Tirmidhi)

This hadith encourages everyone, men and women alike, to seek knowledge and excel in their fields, including business.

Innovation thrives in environments where diverse ideas are encouraged and valued. By promoting gender diversity in entrepreneurship, businesses can harness the full spectrum of creativity and innovation. Women entrepreneurs often spot unique market needs and develop products and services that cater to underserved populations, thus driving market expansion and business growth.

3. **Social Equity and Empowerment**: Economic empowerment is a powerful tool for achieving gender equality. When women have control over economic resources, they gain greater autonomy, better decision-making power within their households, and increased respect in their communities. This kind of empowerment can lead to broader social changes, like improved gender relations and greater social cohesion.

Economic empowerment also helps break the cycle of poverty and dependency. It gives women the means to support themselves and their families, which is especially critical in Muslim-majority countries where gender disparities in education, employment, and income are often pronounced. Promoting entrepreneurship among Muslim women can help create more equitable and just societies.

4. **Role Models and Mentorship**: Successful Muslim women entrepreneurs play a crucial role as role models and mentors for the younger generation, inspiring them to chase their dreams and give back to their communities. Seeing successful women in business challenges stereotypes and shows that they can excel in all fields while staying true to their cultural and religious values.

Mentorship programs totally transform the game for aspiring female entrepreneurs. Experienced businesswomen can provide guidance, share valuable insights, and help navigate the challenges of starting and growing a business. This kind of mentorship creates a supportive ecosystem that encourages more women to dive into entrepreneurship. And it's not just about the business "stuff". These mentors are like beacons of inspiration, helping instil confidence and igniting ambition in young women, showing them that success isn't just a dream – it's within reach.

Challenges Faced by Muslim Women in Business

Despite the undeniable benefits and contributions Muslim women bring to the table, they face a whole set of hurdles holding them back from reaching their full potential. While we'll cover these barriers in more detail later in Chapter 5, the challenges include:

1. **Breaking through Cultural and Societal Barriers**: In many communities, breaking through traditional gender roles and cultural norms is a real struggle for many women in business. Like an invisible barrier holding them back fully, these societal expectations make many women doubt pursuing entrepreneurial activities and fear they will face resistance from their own family and community. There's a whole balancing act between what's expected of them at home and what they want to achieve professionally. Women face resistance not only from their families but also from broader community networks, making it difficult to balance entrepreneurial ambitions with societal expectations. And on top of that? The stigma associated with stepping out of the traditional roles may lead to many women feeling socially isolated and reduce their chances for collaboration and support.

2. **Access to Finance**: Accessing financial resources is another major hurdle for Muslim women entrepreneurs. Banks and financial institutions often have stringent requirements that can be hard to meet, like needing collateral and a solid credit history. Plus, there's often a lack of awareness about other options, like Islamic finance, that might

be a better fit. Discriminatory practices within financial institutions don't help either. Without a solid understanding of financial "stuff" and the various financial instruments available, women's ability to explore viable funding options can be limited.

3. **Networking and Mentorship**: Effective networking and mentorship are crucial for business success, yet many Muslim women lack access to these opportunities. Traditional male-dominated networks and the scarcity of female mentors in business make it tough to connect and learn from others. Without these connections, women often find themselves excluded from informal networks where crucial business information and opportunities are exchanged. This exclusion limits their access to potential investors, partners, and customers. Plus, the lack of visible female role models and mentors in the entrepreneurial space makes it harder for aspiring entrepreneurs to navigate the challenges of starting and growing a business.

4. **Legal and Regulatory Constraints**: In some countries, legal and regulatory frameworks can be big hurdles for women entrepreneurs. Discriminatory laws around property rights, inheritance, and business regulations can make it difficult for women to start and run a business. For instance, discriminatory inheritance laws can prevent women from acquiring capital or assets needed to start a business. Legal restrictions on women's mobility and autonomy can also limit their ability to engage fully in business activities. Moreover, bureaucratic hurdles and corruption can disproportionately affect women, who may have less experience and fewer connections to navigate these challenges effectively.

Opportunities for Muslim Women Entrepreneurs

Despite these hurdles, there are plenty of ways to empower Muslim women in business:

1. **Education and Training**: Tailored education and vocational training can be game-changers. This includes business management cours-

es, financial literacy programs, and technical training in various industries. Specialised programs that tackle the unique challenges faced by women can help build their capacity to succeed in business. Mentorship programs that pair experienced business leaders with aspiring female entrepreneurs can provide valuable guidance and support. Educational initiatives should also focus on digital literacy and technology skills, which are increasingly important in modern business.

2. **Supportive Policies and Initiatives**: Governments and organisations have a crucial role in promoting women's entrepreneurship. This means rolling out policies that support them, like offering grants, low-interest loans, and subsidies and creating women-friendly business environments. Policymakers can also take steps to ensure equal property rights and simplify regulatory processes for women entrepreneurs. By establishing dedicated support centres and providing legal assistance, governments can make it easier for women to navigate the business world. Plus, advocating for women's rights in business forums and raising public awareness can also help shift societal attitudes and encourage greater acceptance of women in business roles.

3. **Islamic Finance**: For many Muslim women entrepreneurs, Islamic finance is a way in. It prohibits interest and emphasises risk-sharing and ethical investments, offering an alternative financing model that aligns with the values of many Muslim women entrepreneurs. Promoting awareness and accessibility of Islamic finance can help bridge the funding gap. Financial institutions should develop products specifically designed for women entrepreneurs, taking into account their unique needs and constraints. Training programs on Islamic finance principles and practices could empower women to make the most of these resources. Collaborating with Islamic banks and microfinance institutions to create dedicated funding programs can make accessing capital even easier.

4. **Technology and Digital Platforms**: The rise of digital technology provides new avenues for women entrepreneurs. Online platforms are opening doors to markets, resources, and networks that were

once out of reach. E-commerce, social media marketing, and digital payment systems are transforming how businesses operate. By leveraging digital tools, women can overcome geographical and societal barriers, reach a global customer base and access resources remotely. Online education platforms offer flexible learning opportunities, while digital networks and forums provide virtual mentorship and support. Encouraging women to participate in tech-based entrepreneurship can also open new fields of innovation and growth.

5. Expanding Networks and Building Communities: Creating networks and communities tailored for Muslim women entrepreneurs can provide essential support and resources. These networks offer opportunities for collaboration, knowledge exchange, and mentorship. By connecting with others who understand their journey, entrepreneurs can share experiences and strategies for overcoming obstacles. Online platforms and social media groups can facilitate these connections, making it easier for women to build supportive professional relationships. And community-based initiatives that encourage women to engage in entrepreneurship, like local business clubs and networking events, can also foster a sense of belonging and empowerment.

6. Enhancing Visibility and Representation: Increasing the visibility of successful Muslim women entrepreneurs can be a powerful tool for inspiration and breaking stereotypes. Media campaigns, awards, and public recognition of women's achievements in business can shine a spotlight on their contributions and potential. Featuring stories of successful female entrepreneurs across various media outlets provides role models for aspiring businesswomen and shows that success is attainable. Encouraging women to take on leadership roles in business associations and advocacy groups can also enhance their influence and visibility in the entrepreneurial community.

Embracing a Future of Inclusive Entrepreneurship

The future of entrepreneurship is inclusive and diverse, with Muslim women playing a pivotal role in shaping it. Embracing this future requires a concerted effort from all stakeholders—governments, financial institutions, educational bodies, and the private sector. By addressing the challenges head-on and leveraging opportunities, we can create an ecosystem that uplifts and celebrates the contributions of Muslim women entrepreneurs.

Prophet Muhammad (pbuh) emphasised the importance of supporting one another in community and business. He said,

> "The believers, in their mutual kindness, compassion, and sympathy, are just like one body. When one of the limbs suffers, the whole body responds to it with wakefulness and fever" (Sahih Bukhari and Muslim)

This hadith reflects the spirit of solidarity and mutual support that should guide our efforts in empowering Muslim women entrepreneurs.

In essence, empowering Muslim women in entrepreneurship isn't just about economic success – it's about achieving social justice and equality. By recognising their potential, breaking down the barriers they face, and providing the necessary support, we can pave the way for a future where Muslim women entrepreneurs thrive and lead the way in innovation, growth, and community development. The journey of empowerment is continuous, requiring the collective commitment of all of us to turn it into a reality.

Inspiring Stories of Successful Muslim Women Entrepreneurs

In this vibrant and ever-evolving world of entrepreneurship, Muslim women are emerging as powerful leaders and innovators. Their stories of resilience, creativity, and success are not only inspiring but also serve as a beacon of hope for many aspiring entrepreneurs. This section delves into the lives and achievements of some trailblazing

Muslim women entrepreneurs who have significantly contributed to their fields. These stories highlight the impact of women's entrepreneurship on economic development and empowerment, providing valuable lessons and motivation for others.

Pioneering Muslim Women Entrepreneurs

Khadijah bint Khuwaylid – The First Entrepreneurial Inspiration

No discussion about successful Muslim women entrepreneurs can begin without mentioning Khadijah bint Khuwaylid, the first wife of Prophet Muhammad (pbuh). Khadijah was a remarkable businesswoman in Makkah who managed a successful caravan trade empire. Her business acumen and integrity set her apart in a predominantly male-dominated society long before she married the Prophet. She was known for her integrity, business acumen, and leadership skills. Her wealth and influence were significant, and she played a crucial role in supporting the early Muslim community.

Khadijah's story is not just one of business success but also one of profound faith and support. She was the first person to believe in Prophet Muhammad's (pbuh) mission, offering him unwavering support both emotionally and financially. Her life showcases the powerful combination of business prowess and spiritual dedication, making her a timeless role model for Muslim women entrepreneurs.

Khadijah's wealth and status were not inherited but earned through hard work and strategic alliances. She employed agents to conduct trade on her behalf, ensuring her goods reached far-off markets like Syria and Yemen. Her success was underpinned by her unwavering commitment to ethical business practices, aligning with the Quranic principle,

"And give full measure and weight in justice and do not deprive the people of their due and do not commit abuse on the earth, spreading corruption" (Quran 11:85)

Khadijah's entrepreneurial spirit was characterised by her ability to negotiate and manage extensive trade operations, securing profits she wisely reinvested into her business. She also employed a large number of people, showcasing her leadership and commitment to providing livelihoods for many.

Khadijah's partnership with Prophet Muhammad (pbuh) is a testament to her entrepreneurial spirit. She recognised his honesty and integrity and entrusted him with her trade caravans, leading to a partnership that thrived economically and also laid the foundation for a deep personal and spiritual relationship. Khadijah's life and legacy serve as a powerful example of how women can excel in business and pursue their entrepreneurial dreams while staying true to their faith and integrity.

Dr Amira Yahyaoui – Tech Innovator and Social Entrepreneur

Dr Amira Yahyaoui is a Tunisian human rights activist and entrepreneur who has made significant strides in the tech industry. She's the brilliant mind behind Mos, a platform that helps students access financial aid and scholarships for higher education. Her journey from activism to entrepreneurship is a testament to her commitment to creating positive social change through technology.

Raised in a politically active family, Amira was exposed to the challenges of her society from a young age. Her experiences fuelled her passion for social justice and innovation. Mos is now a vital resource for countless students, helping to bridge the educational gap and empower young people through access to higher education. Beyond Mos, Dr Yahyaoui continues to advocate for human rights and education, often speaking at international forums and collaborating with global organisations to further her mission. Her innovative approach combines technology with social activism, demonstrating how digital solutions can address deep-rooted societal issues. Her work not only improves access to education but also inspires young entrepreneurs to think beyond profit and focus on social impact.

Huda Kattan – Beauty Mogul and Digital Influencer

Huda Kattan, founder of Huda Beauty, is a prime example of how passion and determination can lead to monumental success. Starting as a beauty blogger, Huda leveraged her online presence to create a global beauty empire. Her brand, known for its high-quality products and innovative marketing strategies, has revolutionised the beauty industry.

Huda's journey began with a passion for makeup and a desire to share her skills with others. Her transparency and relatability endeared her to millions of followers. By understanding her audience and consistently delivering value, Huda turned her personal brand into a thriving business. Today, Huda Beauty is one of the most successful beauty brands worldwide, inspiring countless women to pursue their entrepreneurial dreams.

Her business model incorporates the power of social media to engage directly with customers, garnering a loyal fan base that drives brand loyalty. Huda's success also extends into empowering other women through her beauty academy and mentorship programs, proving that her influence goes beyond cosmetics and fosters a new generation of female entrepreneurs.

Mariam Al Fardous – Medical Doctor and Adventurer

Dr Mariam Al Fardous is not only a successful medical doctor but also an adventurer who has conquered the North Pole. As the first Arab woman to achieve this feat, Mariam has broken numerous barriers and stereotypes. Her achievements in both medicine and exploration exemplify the limitless potential of Muslim women.

Mariam's story is one of courage and perseverance. Balancing a demanding career in medicine with her adventurous pursuits, she has shown that women can excel in diverse fields. Her accomplishments inspire many to push beyond conventional limits and pursue their passions fearlessly.

In addition to her North Pole expedition, Dr Al Fardous advocates for health and wellness, often participating in public speaking events to share her experiences and motivate others. Her dual role as a healthcare provider and an adventurer underscores the diverse capabilities of women and the importance of balancing professional dedication with personal aspirations. She continues to inspire women across the globe to explore new horizons, both literally and metaphorically.

Muna AbuSulayman – Media Personality and Philanthropist

Muna AbuSulayman is a prominent media personality, philanthropist, and co-founder of the Alwaleed Bin Talal Foundation. She has been a strong advocate for women's rights and empowerment in the Middle East. Through her work in media and philanthropy, Muna has made significant contributions to social development and women's empowerment.

Muna's career began in media, where she quickly became a respected voice. Her efforts in promoting social issues and advocating for women's rights have earned her international recognition. As a philanthropist, she has worked tirelessly to support education, healthcare, and economic development programs. Muna's multifaceted career demonstrates the impact of combining media influence with social activism.

Her work with the Alwaleed Bin Talal Foundation involves strategic initiatives aimed at fostering interfaith dialogue, education reform, and humanitarian relief. By leveraging her media platform, she amplifies these efforts, raising awareness and mobilising resources for critical causes. Muna's dedication to social change and ability to navigate and influence various sectors make her a powerful figure in the push for global equity and justice.

Expanding the Impact

These pioneering Muslim women entrepreneurs are breaking barriers and setting new standards in their respective fields. Their stories highlight the importance of resilience, innovation, and faith in overcoming challenges and achieving success. They serve as powerful role models, not only for Muslim women but for all aspiring entrepreneurs globally.

By embracing their heritage and utilising modern tools and platforms, these women are reshaping industries and making impactful contributions to society. Their successes demonstrate that with the right support and opportunities, women can thrive in any field and drive meaningful change. As more Muslim women step into entrepreneurship, they continue to pave the way for future generations, ensuring that the legacy of strong, influential women in business endures and flourishes.

Cheering on and backing more Muslim women to pursue entrepreneurship can shake up communities worldwide in the best way possible. When we tackle their challenges and make the most of the opportunities available, we're not just creating a dynamic global economy; we're crafting a more inclusive world. The successes of these pioneering women underscore the potential for significant social and economic advancements when we knock down barriers and level out the playing field.

Impact of Women's Entrepreneurship on Economic Development & Empowerment

The stories of these successful Muslim women entrepreneurs highlight the transformative power of women's entrepreneurship. Their achievements aren't just about personal victories; they're catalysts for economic development and societal change. By breaking barriers and redefining gender roles, these women pave the way for a more inclusive and equitable society. We'll cover this more in Chapter 7, but for now, let's look at what harnessing the potential of Muslim women in business looks like.

Economic Growth and Job Creation

Women entrepreneurs are essential drivers of economic growth. They create jobs, stimulate local economies, and contribute to the diversification of industries. According to a study by the Global Entrepreneurship Monitor, women are starting businesses at a higher rate than men in many regions, including the Middle East and North Africa. This entrepreneurial activity leads to increased economic stability and prosperity.

For instance, Huda Kattan's Huda Beauty has created numerous jobs within the beauty industry, from product development to marketing and retail. Her company employs a diverse team and has spurred the growth of related businesses, such as beauty supply chains and freelance makeup artists. Similarly, Amira Yahyaoui's Mos provides employment opportunities in the tech sector while addressing critical social needs. By focusing on financial aid for education, Mos creates jobs and invests in the future workforce, contributing to long-term economic growth.

Moreover, women's entrepreneurship often creates more resilient and adaptable businesses. Women tend to reinvest a significant portion of their earnings back into their businesses and communities, fostering sustainable economic growth. This reinvestment can lead to improved infrastructure, better education systems, and enhanced public services, all of which contribute to a more robust economy.

Empowerment and Social Change

Women's entrepreneurship is a powerful tool for social change. It allows women to take control of their economic destinies, lessening dependence on traditional support systems. This empowerment doesn't stop with individuals; it radiates to whole communities. Successful women entrepreneurs often pay it forward, investing in social initiatives and mentoring others.

Muna AbuSulayman's philanthropic efforts are a prime example of how entrepreneurial success can be leveraged for social good. Through her foundation, she supports numerous initiatives to improve education, healthcare, and women's rights, contributing to the overall well-being of her community. Beyond individual impact, her work fosters a culture of giving and social responsibility among other business leaders.

Empowered women entrepreneurs also serve as catalysts for broader social changes. By challenging traditional gender roles, they inspire other women to chase their dreams and stand up for what's rightfully theirs. This ripple effect has the power to drive significant progress – think greater gender equality, reduced poverty, and stronger social cohesion.

Role Models and Mentors

Successful women entrepreneurs serve as role models and mentors for the next generation. Their achievements are tangible proof that women can excel in business and leadership roles, inspiring others to follow in their footsteps. This visibility is crucial in changing societal perceptions and encouraging more women to pursue entrepreneurship.

Khadijah bint Khuwaylid's legacy continues to inspire Muslim women around the world. Her success in business and her unwavering support for Prophet Muhammad (pbuh) demonstrate the potential for women to lead and make significant contributions to society. Modern role models like Huda Kattan and Dr Amira Yahyaoui further reinforce this message, showing that women can achieve remarkable success in diverse fields.

Promoting Gender Equality

Women entrepreneurs are really challenging traditional gender roles and norms. When they succeed in business, they're basically saying "Gender should not be a barrier to success". And that mindset shift is creating a world where everyone, regardless of gender, has a fair shot of success.

Look at Dr Mariam Al Fardous. Her achievements in medicine and exploration challenge conventional stereotypes about women's capabilities. Her success in male-dominated fields serves as a powerful statement about gender equality and women's potential to excel in any domain. By excelling in their respective fields, women entrepreneurs are dismantling the barriers and creating a more level playing field for future generations.

But it's not just about making waves – it's about ensuring the system's fair for everyone. This means pushing for equal access to education, fair pay, and legal protections against discrimination. When we level the playing field and address these systemic issues, we're creating an environment where all individuals have the opportunity to succeed, regardless of gender.

Supporting Community Development

Women entrepreneurs often focus on businesses that address community needs and social issues. Their ventures can lead to improvements in healthcare, education, and other critical areas. By addressing these needs, women entrepreneurs contribute to their communities' overall development and well-being.

Amira Yahyaoui's Mos platform is an excellent example of how a business can tackle major social issues, like access to education. By offering resources for financial aid, Mos is closing the educational gap and empowering the next generation of leaders. This kind of impact is multiplied when successful entrepreneurs invest their time and resources into their communities, creating a cycle of positive change.

What is cool is that women-led businesses often go the extra mile with corporate social responsibility (CSR) initiatives. They're all about sustainable and ethical practices, which can make a big difference – from reducing environmental footprints to improving labour conditions in supply chains. By prioritising CSR, women entrepreneurs are helping build more sustainable and equitable communities.

Lessons Learned from Successful Muslim Women Entrepreneurs

The journeys of these successful Muslim women entrepreneurs have left aspiring entrepreneurs with some valuable lessons. If you're a budding entrepreneur hoping to launch your own business soon, here are some key insights to guide you:

1. **Believe in Your Vision**: A clear vision and unwavering belief in your goals is crucial. Huda Kattan's success with Huda Beauty was driven by her passion for makeup and her belief in the value she could offer her audience.

2. **Leverage Your Unique Strengths**: Each entrepreneur brings unique strengths to their business. Dr Mariam Al Fardous combined her medical expertise with her adventurous spirit to achieve remarkable feats, demonstrating the power of leveraging one's unique qualities.

3. **Seek Knowledge and Stay Informed**: Continuous learning and staying informed about trends in your industry are essential for success. Khadijah bint Khuwaylid's business acumen was enhanced by her deep understanding of trade and commerce.

4. **Persevere Through Challenges**: Resilience is key to overcoming obstacles. Amira Yahyaoui's transition from activism to entrepreneurship required perseverance and adaptability, which helped her succeed in the tech industry.

5. **Give Back to Your Community**: Successful entrepreneurs often give back to their communities. Muna AbuSulayman's philanthropic efforts show the importance of using success to support and uplift others.

6. **Build a Strong Support Network**: Surrounding yourself with supportive individuals can make a significant difference. Huda Kattan's success was bolstered by the support of her family and her ability to build a loyal community of followers.

By learning from these trailblazers, aspiring entrepreneurs (maybe like you!) can navigate their journeys with confidence and determination. These lessons highlight the importance of vision, resilience, continuous learning, and community support in achieving entrepreneurial success.

Women's entrepreneurship not only benefits individuals; it has a profound impact on economic development and empowerment. By fostering an inclusive environment that supports and encourages women entrepreneurs, societies can unlock significant economic and social benefits. As more women step into entrepreneurial roles, they'll continue to drive innovation, create jobs, and inspire future generations, contributing to a more prosperous and equitable world.

Conclusion

The stories of successful Muslim women entrepreneurs are a testament to the power of resilience, innovation, and faith. These women have not only achieved personal success but have also made significant contributions to their communities and the broader society. Their journeys offer invaluable lessons and inspiration for aspiring entrepreneurs, highlighting the transformative impact of women's entrepreneurship on economic development and empowerment.

By celebrating and supporting Muslim women entrepreneurs, we can foster a more inclusive and equitable global economy. The achievements of these trailblazing women serve as a reminder that with determination, faith, and the right support, anything is possible. As we look to the future, let's continue to empower and uplift Muslim women entrepreneurs, ensuring their contributions are recognised and celebrated, paving the way for a brighter and more prosperous future for all.

Chapter Two

Prophet Muhammad as an Entrepreneur

Business Ventures of Prophet Muhammad (pbuh)

In the vast tapestry of Islamic history, Prophet Muhammad (pbuh) stands as a towering figure whose life and actions offer timeless lessons. Among his many roles, his endeavours in trade and commerce provide profound insights into ethical business practices and the principles that can guide modern entrepreneurs. The Prophet's ventures were marked by honesty, integrity, and a commitment to fairness, attributes that are as relevant today as they were in 7th century Arabia. This chapter delves into the business ventures of Prophet Muhammad (pbuh), exploring the lessons that contemporary entrepreneurs can draw from his example.

Examples of the Prophet's involvement in trade and commerce

Early Life and Involvement in Trade

Prophet Muhammad (pbuh) was born into the Quraysh tribe of Mecca, a bustling hub of trade and commerce. From a young age, he was involved in the trading activities of his family. His early exposure to the world of business laid the foundation for his later success as a trader.

Even before his prophethood, Prophet Muhammad (pbuh) was known for his trustworthy nature, earning him the nickname Al-Amin, meaning "the trustworthy." This reputation was a critical asset in a society where trust and reliability were paramount in trade. His character was a living testament to the Quranic principle,

> "And fulfil the covenant. Indeed, the covenant will be questioned about" (Quran 17:34)

This emphasis on trust and fulfilling agreements is a cornerstone of ethical business practices.

From a young age, Prophet Muhammad (pbuh) accompanied his uncle Abu Talib on business journeys. These experiences taught him practical knowledge and exposed him to different trading practices and cultures. His knack for picking things up quickly meant he got the hang of the nuances of commerce and the importance of maintaining ethical standards in business. As he grew older, he took on more responsibilities in trade, handling transactions solo and building his reputation for honesty and fairness.

The Business Partnership with Khadijah

One of the most significant phases of Prophet Muhammad's (pbuh) business career was his partnership with Khadijah bint Khuwaylid, who later became his wife. Khadijah was a successful and wealthy businesswoman who owned extensive trade caravans that travelled across the Arabian Peninsula. Recognising Prophet Muhammad's (pbuh) integrity and skill, she employed him to manage her trade expeditions.

With Prophet Muhammad (pbuh) at the helm, Khadijah's business flourished. His honesty and fairness in dealing with clients and partners increased profits and enhanced the reputation of Khadijah's enterprise. Their partnership was built on mutual respect and trust—Khadijah provided capital and resources, while Prophet Muhammad (pbuh) brought his expertise and ethical conduct. This collaboration exemplifies the Islamic principle of Shura, or mutual consultation, which is key for successful partnerships.

Khadijah's trust in Prophet Muhammad (pbuh) grew even deeper when she proposed marriage to him, impressed by his character and business acumen. Their marriage was a true partnership in every sense, combining Khadijah's financial smarts and Prophet Muhammad's (pbuh) managerial skills. Together, they navigated the challenges of the trade business, always ensuring that their operations were ethical and efficient. Their union not only set a precedent for successful business collaborations but also highlighted the significant role of women in commerce, challenging societal norms of the time.

Key Business Principles from the Prophet's Ventures

1. **Honesty and Integrity**: One of the standout features of Prophet Muhammad's (pbuh) business dealings was his unwavering honesty. In every transaction, he upheld the highest standards of truthfulness. He once said,

> "The truthful and trustworthy merchant is with the Prophets, the truthful, and the martyrs" (Al-Tirmidhi)

This hadith underscores the immense value placed on honesty in Islam, particularly in business.

Prophet Muhammad's (pbuh) commitment to honesty was clear in his transparent dealings. He would openly disclose the quality and condition of the goods he sold, making sure buyers knew exactly what they were getting. This practice built trust and loyalty among his clients, setting a standard for ethical business conduct. His reputation for honesty was so well-established that even those who opposed him couldn't deny his integrity. This principle of truthfulness remains a cornerstone for Muslim entrepreneurs today, guiding them to maintain transparency and build long-lasting relationships with their customers.

2. **Fair Dealing and Justice**: Prophet Muhammad (pbuh) was known for his fair dealings. He ensured all parties involved in a transaction got what they deserved and were treated fairly. This principle is echoed in the Quran,

> "And give full measure when you measure, and weigh with an even balance. That is the best [way] and best in result" (Quran 17:35)

This idea about fairness isn't just about trust; it's about making sure business relationships last.

Prophet Muhammad's emphasis on justice extended to every aspect of his business; it permeated everything he did. He was meticulous in ensuring that weights and measures were accurate, a practice that was critical in maintaining fairness in trade. He also advocated for fair pricing, avoiding excessive markups that could exploit customers. This didn't just earn him a good reputation; it built a sense of trust and reliability, bringing in more customers and ensuring they came back. The principle of justice in trade isn't just a historical lesson; it's a key to ethical dealings and long-term success today.

3. **Customer Satisfaction**: Prophet Muhammad (pbuh) always prioritised customers' happiness. He believed their contentment was crucial for business success. His words,

> "May Allah have mercy on the one who is lenient in his buying, selling, and in demanding back his money" (Sahih Bukhari)

This kindness and understanding of his customers created a bond of loyalty and encouraged them to come back time and time again.

He strongly believed in listening to his customers. He was known for being approachable and attentive, always ready to go the extra mile to ensure they left happy. For contemporary businesses, focusing on customer satisfaction is key to building a loyal customer base and ensuring sustained growth.

4. **Ethical Profit-Making**: While profit is a natural objective of any business, Prophet Muhammad (pbuh) emphasised ethical profit-making. He discouraged deceit and exploitation, advocating for profits earned through fair and transparent means. This principle is highlighted in the Quran,

> "O you who have believed, do not consume one another's wealth unjustly or send it [in bribery] to the rulers in order that [they might aid] you [to] consume a portion of the wealth of the people in sin, while you know [it is unlawful]" (Quran 2:188)

Prophet Muhammad's (pbuh) business practices reflected a balance between making a profit and maintaining ethical standards. He rejected any form of deceit. Prioritising ethical profit-making meant that his business practices were sustainable and built on trust. This principle holds immense relevance today, as businesses face increasing scrutiny for their ethical practices by both consumers and stakeholders.

Business Trips to Syria and Beyond

One of the journeys that left a lasting mark on the life of Prophet Muhammad (pbuh) were his business trips to Syria. These trips were pivotal in expanding his knowledge of trade and commerce and shaping his reputation as a reliable and honest trader. Venturing into various markets, he immersed himself in different cultures and trading practices. This exposure helped him develop a keen understanding of market dynamics and customer behaviour.

During these trips, Prophet Muhammad's (pbuh) fair dealing and truthful nature stood out. He always ensured that he bought goods at fair prices and sold them with reasonable profit margins. His ethical practices drew more clients and established a loyal customer base, which is a testament to the saying of the Prophet,

> "The best earnings are from a sale where there is no cheating or fraud" (Al-Tirmidhi)

Beyond enhancing his ethical business practices, these business trips broadened Prophet Muhammad's (pbuh) perspective on international trade practices. From observing the diverse business strategies of those traders, he was able to implement the best of those practices in his trade dealings. The lessons from his travels underscore the importance of continuous learning, cultural sensitivity, and ethical practices for modern entrepreneurs striving for long-term success.

Lessons for Modern Entrepreneurs

If you're an entrepreneur, the business ventures of Prophet Muhammad (pbuh) offer timeless lessons that are invaluable for today's business landscape. These lessons, rooted in ethical conduct and social responsibility, are essential to you for building sustainable and successful businesses.

1. **Build a Reputation of Trust**: Trust is the cornerstone of any successful business. It's important you strive to build and maintain a reputation for honesty and reliability. How? Well, start by being upfront and transparent in all dealings and consistently deliver on promises. When people see you as trustworthy, you'll attract loyal customers, reliable partners, and a dedicated team. In today's digital age, where information spreads rapidly, maintaining integrity in business practices is more crucial than ever. Trust, once broken, can be challenging to rebuild, so keeping it real and honest is key. Implementing robust ethical guidelines and ensuring your team adheres to them will go a long way in sustaining a trustworthy reputation.

2. **Prioritise Customer Satisfaction**: As a modern entrepreneur, ensuring customer satisfaction should be your primary goal. This means really understanding what your customers need, delivering high-quality products and services, and being fair and lenient in transactions. Happy customers not only keep coming back but are more likely to return and recommend your business to others. Why not use tools like customer feedback surveys and social media to stay on top of how they're feeling and address any issues promptly? Going the extra mile with exceptional customer service, offering value beyond the product, and making each interaction personal can really win hearts. If any issues do come up, resolve them with care and speed, showing customers just how much you value their satisfaction.

3. **Engage in Fair Trade Practices**: Fairness in trade practices isn't just about a good reputation – it's about making sure your business can thrive in the long term. As an entrepreneur, avoid deceitful practices, ensure fair pricing, and treat all stakeholders fairly. This means not only adhering to ethical standards but promoting transparency every step of the way, from supply chains to the entire business process. Fair trade means paying fair wages, ensuring safe working conditions, and sourcing materials ethically. By committing to fair trade, you're contributing to a more equitable economy and building stronger relationships with your suppliers and customers. Plus, in a market where

ethics matter, it's a great way to stand out and attract consumers who care where their products come from.

4. **Embrace Ethical Profit-Making**: Profits should be earned through ethical means. That means avoiding exploitation, being transparent about product quality and pricing, and ensuring that business practices align with moral and ethical standards. By being upfront and honest, your business will grow in a way that's sustainable and fosters a positive corporate image. This involves implementing clear ethical guidelines, providing training and ensuring everyone on your team understands and adheres to these standards. And why stop there? Your priority should also be corporate social responsibility (CSR), which means investing in your community and contributing to building a sustainable environment. Ethical profit-making also means avoiding practices that harm society, such as exploiting labour or engaging in corrupt activities. By prioritising ethics, your business can achieve long-term success and maintain a positive reputation.

5. **Seek Knowledge and Continuous Improvement**: Just as Prophet Muhammad (pbuh) gained valuable insights from his trade journeys, as a modern entrepreneur, it's important you continuously seek knowledge and opportunities for improvement. This can be through formal education, market research, or learning from industry peers. Staying informed about industry trends, technological advancements, and consumer behaviour helps you stay ahead of the game. So why not invest in yourself and your team? Invest in professional development for you and your team, encouraging a culture of continuous learning. This could be attending workshops, seminars, and industry conferences, as well as subscribing to relevant publications. When you make knowledge and growth a priority, you're setting yourself up to tackle whatever the changing market conditions throw your way.

6. **Foster Partnerships and Collaboration**: The Prophet's partnership with Khadijah highlights the importance of collaboration. As an entrepreneur, it's all about finding mutually beneficial partnerships. That means engaging in Shura (consultation) and respecting the con-

tributions of all partners. Collaboration opens doors to new markets, resources, and expertise, helping your business grow and become more creative. But it's not only about making deals – it's about building strong, respectful relationships with partners, suppliers, and stakeholders. This means open communication, shared goals, and mutual trust. Joint ventures, strategic alliances, and cooperative networks can help your business expand its reach and capabilities. Actively participating in industry associations and community groups is also key to building a supportive business ecosystem.

The Broader Impact of the Prophet's Business Ethics

The ethical business practices of Prophet Muhammad (pbuh) had far-reaching impacts beyond his personal success. They set a standard for the Muslim community and established principles that continue to guide Islamic business ethics today. His emphasis on honesty, fairness, and social responsibility resonates with contemporary movements towards ethical and sustainable business practices.

In today's globalised world, where businesses are often driven by profit maximisation at the expense of ethical considerations, Prophet Muhammad's (pbuh) example reminds us of the importance of integrity and social responsibility in commerce. Businesses that adhere to these principles are more likely to gain the trust and loyalty of their customers, employees, and communities, leading to long-term success and sustainability.

Ethical business practices also contribute to a positive corporate culture, attracting talent and fostering employee loyalty. By prioritising ethical behaviour, businesses can create a work environment that values integrity, fairness, and respect. This not only enhances employee satisfaction but also boosts productivity and innovation.

Conclusion

Prophet Muhammad's (pbuh) business ventures are a rich source of guidance for modern entrepreneurs. His life exemplifies how ethical business practices can lead to success and positive social impact. By emulating his principles of honesty, fairness, customer satisfaction, and ethical profit-making, we can build businesses that are not only successful but also contribute to society's well-being.

In an age where ethical considerations are becoming increasingly important to consumers and stakeholders, the timeless wisdom of Prophet Muhammad (pbuh) offers a valuable framework for conducting business. His example encourages us to view business as a means of earning profits but as a platform for promoting trust, justice, and social good.

As we navigate the complexities of the modern business world, let's draw inspiration from Prophet Muhammad's (pbuh) ventures and strive to uphold the highest standards of integrity and ethics in our entrepreneurial endeavours. By doing so, we can achieve true success that benefits not only ourselves but also our communities and the world at large.

Ultimately, Prophet Muhammad's (pbuh) teachings remind us that true business success is not measured solely by financial gain but by our positive impact on others. By embracing these timeless principles as entrepreneurs, we can create sustainable, ethical businesses that contribute to a better world.

Prophetic Guidelines for Entrepreneurship

The life of Prophet Muhammad (pbuh) offers an enduring legacy of ethical conduct, integrity, and profound wisdom. These qualities were not only reflected in his spiritual and social teachings but also in his approach to business and entrepreneurship. For contemporary Muslim entrepreneurs, Prophet Muhammad's (pbuh) guidelines provide a framework that can lead to both material success and spiritual fulfilment. This chapter explores the principles of Sunnah applicable to modern business endeavours, emphasising honesty, integrity, and fair dealings.

The Sunnah Principles Applicable to Modern Business

Entrepreneurship, at its core, is about innovation, risk-taking, and value creation. However, for Muslim entrepreneurs, it also involves adhering to the moral and ethical guidelines laid out by Prophet Muhammad (pbuh). These guidelines encompass various aspects of business, from personal conduct to dealing with employees and customers.

> Prophet Muhammad (pbuh) said, "The best of you are those who have the best character" (Sahih Bukhari)

This hadith underscores the importance of character and ethics in all aspects of life, including business. An entrepreneur with good character is trustworthy, honest, and fair, qualities that are essential for building a reputable and sustainable business.

Honesty and Integrity

One of the most emphasised principles in Prophet Muhammad's teachings is honesty. In a business context, this means being truthful in all dealings, whether advertising products, setting prices, or negotiating contracts. The Quran states,

> "O you who have believed, fear Allah and be with those who are true" (Quran 9:119)

This verse encourages Muslims to embody truthfulness in all their actions.

Long before he received prophethood, Prophet Muhammad (pbuh) was known as Al-Amin (the trustworthy). His reputation for honesty was a cornerstone of his business success. For example, when managing the trade caravans for Khadijah, he ensured that all transactions were transparent and fair, significantly boosting the business's reputation and profitability.

Modern entrepreneurs can learn from this by maintaining transparency in their operations. This means being clear and honest in all communications with stakeholders, avoiding misleading claims about products or services, and ensuring that all financial dealings are straightforward and documented. Building a business on a foundation of honesty not only attracts loyal customers but also fosters long-term partnerships and investments.

Fair Dealings and Justice

Justice and fairness are integral to Islamic teachings. The Quran instructs,

> "And weigh with an even balance" (Quran 55:9)

This verse highlights the importance of fairness in trade and business. Prophet Muhammad (pbuh) consistently advocated for the just treatment of all individuals, including customers, employees, and business partners.

In practice, this means ensuring that all business transactions are just. For instance, setting fair prices that reflect the true value of goods and services, providing accurate product information, and treating employees fairly by paying them on time and respecting their rights. Prophet Muhammad (pbuh) said,

> "Give the worker his wages before his sweat dries" (Ibn Majah)

This hadith emphasises the importance of timely and fair compensation for employees.

Trust and Reliability

Trust is a crucial element in any business relationship. Prophet Muhammad (pbuh) emphasised the importance of fulfilling promises and maintaining trustworthiness. He said,

> "The signs of a hypocrite are three: whenever he speaks, he tells a lie; whenever he promises, he breaks it; and whenever he is entrusted, he betrays" (Sahih Bukhari)

For entrepreneurs, this means delivering on promises to customers, partners, and employees. Whether it's a product delivery deadline, a service commitment, or a financial obligation, fulfilling these promises builds trust and enhances the business's reputation. Trustworthiness is a key differentiator in a competitive market and can lead to repeat business and customer loyalty.

Ethical Profit-Making

While profit is a natural and essential goal of any business, Islam places significant emphasis on how profits are earned. The Quran advises,

> "O you who have believed, do not consume one another's wealth unjustly or send it [in bribery] to the rulers in order that [they might aid] you [to] consume a portion of the wealth of the people in sin, while you know [it is unlawful]" (Quran 2:188)

This verse highlights the prohibition of unjust and unethical methods of earning.

Prophet Muhammad (pbuh) encouraged fair trade practices and condemned exploitation and deceit. He said,

> "Whoever cheats us is not one of us" (Sahih Muslim)

This strong stance against fraud and deception underlines the importance of ethical behaviour in all business dealings. Entrepreneurs should strive to earn profits through honest and ethical means, avoiding practices that exploit or deceive customers or employees.

Social Responsibility and Charity

Islamic teachings also emphasise the importance of social responsibility and charity. The concept of Zakat, one of the five pillars of Islam, mandates Muslims to give a portion of their wealth to those in need. This principle extends to business practices, where entrepreneurs are encouraged to contribute to the welfare of society.

Prophet Muhammad (pbuh) was renowned for his generosity and concern for the less fortunate. He said,

> "The believer's shade on the Day of Resurrection will be his charity" (Tirmidhi)

Modern entrepreneurs can embody this principle through corporate social responsibility (CSR) initiatives. This might involve supporting local communities, adopting environmentally sustainable practices, and contributing to charitable causes. These actions not only fulfil a religious obligation but also enhance the business's reputation and strengthen community ties.

Innovation and Adaptability

While Prophet Muhammad's (pbuh) era vastly differed from today's fast-paced business environment, his approach to problem-solving and innovation remains relevant. He demonstrated adaptability and foresight in his business dealings. For example, he recognised and capitalised on the trade routes and market demands of his time, ensuring the success of the trade caravans he managed.

In today's world, entrepreneurs must embrace innovation and adaptability to stay competitive. This involves staying informed about industry trends, leveraging new technologies, and continuously improving products and services. Adapting to changing market conditions and customer needs is crucial for long-term business success.

Empowerment and Inclusion

Prophet Muhammad (pbuh) advocated for the empowerment of all individuals, regardless of gender, social status, or ethnicity. His marriage to Khadijah, a successful businesswoman, and his support for her business endeavours exemplify his progressive views on women's economic participation. He said,

> "Seek knowledge from the cradle to the grave" (Al-Tabarani)

Thereby encouraging both men and women to pursue education and personal development.

For modern entrepreneurs, this means creating inclusive business environments that empower all employees and stakeholders. Encouraging diversity and equal opportunities for all individuals can lead to a more innovative and dynamic business. Moreover, supporting women's entrepreneurship and leadership within the business community can drive broader economic growth and social progress.

Conclusion

The prophetic guidelines for entrepreneurship, rooted in honesty, integrity, and social responsibility, offer a timeless framework for building successful and ethical businesses. By adhering to these principles, Muslim entrepreneurs can achieve financial success, spiritual fulfilment, and social impact.

In a world where business practices are often driven by profit maximisation and competitive pressures, Prophet Muhammad's (pbuh) example is a powerful reminder of the importance of ethical conduct and social responsibility. His teachings encourage us to view business as a means of contributing to the well-being of society, fostering trust, and promoting justice.

As we navigate the complexities of the modern business landscape, let's draw inspiration from Prophet Muhammad's (pbuh) guidelines and strive to uphold the highest standards of ethics and integrity in our entrepreneurial endeavours. By doing so, we can build businesses that not only succeed financially but make a positive difference in the world.

Chapter Three

Women Entrepreneurs in Islamic History

Contributions of Muslim Women in Business

Stories of pioneering female entrepreneurs in early Islamic societies

In the rich tapestry of Islamic history, Muslim women have played a crucial role in shaping the economic landscape. Their contributions to business and commerce have not only driven economic growth but have also defied societal norms and paved the way for future generations. This section explores the stories of pioneering female entrepreneurs in early Islamic societies, shedding light on their obstacles and remarkable achievements. Through their resilience and ingenuity, these women have left an indelible mark on the world of entrepreneurship, carrying forward the legacy of Khadijah bint Khuwaylid.

Fatimah al-Fihri: Founder of the World's First University

Another pioneering figure in Islamic history is Fatimah al-Fihri, a remarkable woman who founded the University of al-Qarawiyyin in Fez, Morocco, in 859 AD. This institution is considered the world's oldest continuously operating university. Fatimah, born into a wealthy family, used her inheritance to establish this learning centre, reflecting her commitment to education and intellectual growth.

The establishment of al-Qarawiyyin was not merely an act of philanthropy but a strategic investment in the future of her community. Fatimah's vision extended beyond the immediate economic benefits, aiming to foster knowledge, cultural exchange, and scholarly advancement. Her legacy is a powerful reminder of the transformative impact of education and the pivotal role women can play in shaping intellectual and cultural landscapes.

Fatimah's initiative to create al-Qarawiyyin also emphasised the importance of accessible education. She made sure that the university was open to people of diverse backgrounds, fostering an environment of inclusivity and intellectual diversity. The curriculum offered at al-Qarawiyyin covered many subjects, including religious studies, mathematics, medicine, astronomy, and philosophy. Her approach to education contributed significantly to the intellectual and cultural development of the region. Al-Qarawiyyin attracted students from across the Islamic world and Europe, facilitating a rich exchange of knowledge and ideas. Fatimah's dedication to education and innovative methods in establishing a sustainable learning institution has left a lasting legacy that inspires educational advancements today.

Lubna of Córdoba: Scholar and Administrator

In the 10th century, Lubna of Córdoba emerged as a significant figure in the intellectual and administrative spheres of the Umayyad Caliphate in Spain. Initially a slave, Lubna's exceptional intellect and skills in mathematics, grammar, and calligraphy led to her emancipation and subsequent rise to prominence. She became the chief scribe and personal secretary to Caliph Al-Hakam II, overseeing the vast library of Córdoba.

Lubna's contributions went beyond her administrative duties. She was instrumental in copying, translating, and preserving many important manuscripts, playing a critical role in the intellectual life of the caliphate. Her story illustrates how Muslim women, even in constrained circumstances, could rise to positions of influence and make significant contributions to society.

Lubna's journey from slavery to a prominent intellectual position is a testament to her determination and exceptional talents. Her work in the library of Córdoba, which housed one of the largest collections of books in the medieval world, was vital in preserving and disseminating knowledge. The library contained works in various fields, such as science, medicine, philosophy, and literature. Lubna's meticulous work ensured that these manuscripts were accurately copied and preserved for future generations. Her role also included facilitating scholarly exchanges and acquiring new works, further enriching the library's collection. Lubna's legacy is a powerful example of how education and intellectual pursuits can transcend social barriers and significantly impact cultural and scholarly development.

Zaynab al-Shahda: The Calligrapher and Scholar

In the medieval Islamic world, Zaynab al-Shahda was renowned for her expertise in calligraphy and scholarship. She lived during the Abbasid Caliphate and was highly respected for her knowledge and artistic skills. Zaynab's work was not limited to calligraphy; she also taught and mentored other scholars, contributing to the intellectual and cultural heritage of her time.

Zaynab's prominence in a male-dominated field highlights the potential for women to excel in various disciplines. Her dedication to her craft and ability to balance her professional and personal life inspire contemporary women striving to make their mark in the business world.

Zaynab al-Shahda's calligraphic works were highly sought after and valued for their precision and beauty. Her expertise in calligraphy went beyond mere artistic expression; it played a critical role in the documentation and dissemination of knowledge. The manuscripts she produced included religious texts, scientific works, and literary pieces, all of which contributed to the rich tapestry of Islamic scholarship. Zaynab was also a respected teacher who trained numerous students, ensuring her skills and knowledge were passed on to future generations. Her commitment to mentoring and educating others helped foster a community of scholars and artists, enriching the cultural heritage of the Abbasid Caliphate. Zaynab's legacy underscores the importance of artistic and intellectual pursuits and the vital role women have played in advancing these fields.

Broader Impacts and Legacy

The stories of Fatimah al-Fihri, Lubna of Córdoba, and Zaynab al-Shahda illustrate the significant impact that Muslim women have had on education, intellectual life, and the arts throughout history. Their achievements demonstrate that women have long played crucial roles in shaping cultural and intellectual landscapes despite the societal constraints they often faced.

These pioneering women serve as powerful role models for contemporary women, inspiring them to pursue their passions and contribute to their fields. Their legacies remind us of the importance of education, intellectual curiosity, and the arts in advancing society. By celebrating and learning from these historical figures, we can continue to support and empower women in all areas of life, fostering a more inclusive and equitable world.

The contributions of these remarkable women are a testament to the enduring influence of female leadership and innovation in Islamic history. Their dedication to knowledge, cultural exchange, and intellectual advancement has left a lasting impact that continues to inspire future generations. As we reflect on their stories, we're reminded of the transformative power of education and the pivotal role women can play in shaping the future. By upholding their legacy and promoting the values they embody, we can ensure that the contributions of women are recognised and celebrated in all spheres of life.

Challenges Faced by Muslim Businesswomen

Despite their remarkable achievements, these pioneering women faced significant challenges. Societal norms and gender biases limited their opportunities and recognition. However, their resilience and determination empowered them to overcome these obstacles and thrive in their respective fields.

1. **Societal Norms and Gender Bias**: In many early Islamic societies, women were expected to confine themselves to domestic roles. Stepping into the public sphere and engaging in business required overcoming deeply entrenched societal expectations. Women like Khadijah and Fatimah defied these norms, proving that women could excel in business and intellectual pursuits. They faced scepticism and resistance from their communities, but their unwavering resolve helped them break those barriers. These women had to navigate a landscape where their abilities were often underestimated, and their successes were scrutinised more harshly than those of their male counterparts.

2. **Access to Education and Resources**: Another major obstacle for these women was their limited access to education and resources. Fatimah al-Fihri's ability to establish a university was facilitated by her family's wealth and her personal commitment to education. For many women, gaining the knowledge and skills necessary for business and intellectual pursuits was a considerable hurdle. In many cases, societal structures limited their access to formal education and financial resources. So, women who aspired to learn had to find ways around these structural barriers by being resourceful, getting support from their families, and building connections in their communities.

3. **Recognition and Influence**: Gaining recognition and influence in male-dominated fields was an uphill battle. Women like Lubna and Zaynab had to demonstrate exceptional skill and knowledge just to be acknowledged and respected by their male counterparts. Their success paved the way for future generations of women. But, despite their contributions, these women often had to work twice as hard to

receive half the recognition. Their stories show how women still have to prove themselves in environments where their presence isn't traditionally valued. Despite all the challenges, their ability to command respect and influence is a testament to their extraordinary resilience and talent.

Achievements and Legacy

The achievements of these pioneering Muslim women entrepreneurs extend beyond their immediate successes. They have left a lasting legacy that continues to inspire and empower women worldwide.

1. Economic Contributions: Women like Khadijah significantly contributed to the economic prosperity of their communities. By engaging in trade and commerce, she created jobs, stimulated economic activity, and fostered trade relations with other regions. Her wealth and business savvy provided financial stability for her family and supported the early Muslim community. Her investments and business ventures opened doors for many, demonstrating the critical role women can play in driving economic development. This legacy of economic contribution underscores the importance of inclusive participation in commerce and trade.

2. Educational and Intellectual Advancements: The establishment of institutions like the University of al-Qarawiyyin by Fatimah al-Fihri and the scholarly contributions of Lubna and Zaynab have profoundly impacted the intellectual development of Islamic societies. These women played a crucial role in preserving and advancing knowledge. Fatimah al-Fihri's vision for al-Qarawiyyin as a centre for learning has endured for centuries, influencing educational practices globally. Lubna's meticulous work in preserving and disseminating knowledge ensured that critical scholarly works were accessible to future generations. Their commitment to education and scholarship set a high standard for academic excellence and intellectual pursuit.

3. **Cultural and Artistic Heritage**: The work of women like Zaynab al-Shahda in calligraphy and the arts has enriched the cultural heritage of the Islamic world. Their contributions to literature, art, and scholarship continue to be celebrated and studied today. Zaynab's artistic excellence in calligraphy not only preserved important texts but also elevated the art form to new heights. Her mentorship of other scholars ensured that her skills and knowledge were passed down, enriching the cultural and artistic landscape of her time.

4. **Inspiration for Future Generations**: Perhaps the most enduring legacy of these pioneering women is the inspiration they provide for future generations. Their stories of resilience, innovation, and success serve as powerful role models for young women aspiring to make their mark in business and other fields. The enduring impact of their achievements continues to motivate women to pursue their ambitions despite societal challenges. These trailblazers have shown that with determination, education, and ethical practices, women can achieve extraordinary success and contribute significantly to their communities and beyond.

Lessons for Modern Muslim Women Entrepreneurs

The stories of these pioneering women entrepreneurs offer valuable lessons to contemporary Muslim women looking to navigate the world of business. If you're a female entrepreneur, the following insights will be of value to you:

1. **Embrace Resilience and Determination**: The path to success is rarely straightforward. Khadijah and Fatimah al-Fihri faced numerous hurdles on their path to success, yet they persevered in the face of challenges. Their stories teach us the value of cultivating a mindset that embraces challenges as opportunities for growth and to remain steadfast in the pursuit of our goals. Cultivating resilience is critical in navigating the complexities and uncertainties of the business world.

2. **Leverage Education and Knowledge**: Fatimah and Lubna's commitment to education highlights the power of knowledge in opening doors to new opportunities and empowering women to excel in their chosen fields. Investing in your education and seeking new knowledge and skill development is essential for staying competitive and innovative in today's rapidly evolving business environment. Seek out educational opportunities, mentors, and resources to sharpen your abilities and remain competitive in the ever-evolving market.

3. **Uphold Ethical Practices**: Khadijah's ethical business approach and Zaynab al-Shahda's commitment to scholarly integrity serve as shining examples of the importance of maintaining high ethical standards. In today's world, maintaining high ethical standards is not just commendable – it's crucial. From sourcing materials to marketing practices, prioritising integrity and honesty is the foundation for a sustainable and respected business. By upholding strong ethical principles, you're choosing to cultivate trust and loyalty among your customers, team, and stakeholders.

4. **Seek Mentorship and Support**: Just as these pioneering women drew strength from their families and communities, you, too, can benefit from mentors and supporters. Surrounding yourself with experienced mentors who believe in your vision provides insights, advice, and support to navigate the challenges of entrepreneurship. A strong support network offers emotional and practical assistance, fueling your motivation and resilience in adversity.

5. **Balance Professional and Personal Life**: Finding harmony between your professional and personal life is crucial. Women like Zaynab excelled in their professional endeavours while managing personal responsibilities. This should serve as a reminder of the importance of balance and self-care. As a modern entrepreneur, prioritising your well-being and striving for a healthy work-life balance is essential. Effective time management, delegating tasks, and setting boundaries are essential strategies for maintaining this balance. Nurturing

your physical and mental health is crucial for sustained success and fulfilment.

6. **Innovate and Adapt**: Embracing innovation and adaptability is indispensable for remaining relevant in today's rapidly changing world. Drawing inspiration from the pioneering women of Islamic history, who were able to innovate and adapt to the challenges of their time, is a lesson that remains pertinent today. Embracing change and being open to new ideas and technologies, market trends, customer needs, and technological advancements can give you a competitive edge. Remember, innovation involves creating new products and services and continually refining more efficient and effective ways to operate and grow your business.

Conclusion

The contributions of Muslim women to business and entrepreneurship in Islamic history are both inspiring and instructive. Their resilience, innovation, and success stories provide valuable lessons for contemporary Muslim women entrepreneurs. By embracing the principles of integrity, knowledge, and perseverance, you can build on this rich legacy and continue propelling economic growth and social change forward.

The journey of Muslim women in business is a testament to the enduring power of faith, resilience, and innovation. By drawing inspiration from the past and embracing the opportunities of the present, Muslim women entrepreneurs, perhaps like you, can forge a path towards a brighter and more equitable future.

Empowering Muslimah Entrepreneurs Today

Empowering Muslim women entrepreneurs today is a continuation of a rich historical tradition and a pressing necessity in the modern global economy. As we look to the inspiring examples of the past, we also need to focus on the present opportunities and challenges that

Muslim women face in business. This chapter will explore strategies for supporting women's entrepreneurship through education and opportunities and promoting gender equality and economic empowerment in Muslim communities. By drawing on Islamic principles and modern best practices, we can create a more inclusive and dynamic entrepreneurial ecosystem.

Supporting women's entrepreneurship through education and opportunities

Education is a cornerstone of empowerment, and this is particularly true for entrepreneurship. Prophet Muhammad (pbuh) said,

> "Seeking knowledge is an obligation upon every Muslim" (Sunan Ibn Majah)

This emphasis on the pursuit of knowledge underscores the importance of education for both men and women in Islam. For Muslim women entrepreneurs, access to quality education and training is essential for developing the skills and confidence needed to succeed in business.

Formal Education and Vocational Training

One of the most effective ways to empower Muslim women entrepreneurs is through formal education and vocational training. Educational institutions can play a pivotal role by offering courses in business management, finance, marketing, and technology tailored to women's needs. These programs should be accessible and affordable, ensuring that women who want to learn can.

That's not all. Vocational training programs are equally important—hands-on practical skills like accounting, digital marketing, customer service, and product development. Equipping women with these skills enables them to manage their businesses more effectively and compete in the global marketplace. And, of course, equally important is removing the financial barrier. Creating scholarships and financial aid programs specifically for women can really help knock down those economic barriers to education.

Mentorship and Networking

Mentorship and networking are critical components of entrepreneurial success. For Muslim women entrepreneurs, finding mentors who understand their unique challenges and perspectives can make a huge difference.

And then there's networking – business conferences, workshops, and industry events allow women to connect with other entrepreneurs, potential partners, and investors. These interactions can lead to collaborations, partnerships, and new business opportunities. Creating networks specifically for Muslim women entrepreneurs can foster community and mutual support. Online platforms and social media groups are also great for building these networks, providing a space for women to share resources, advice, and encouragement.

Access to Financial Resources

Access to finance is often a big roadblock for women entrepreneurs. Traditional financial institutions often have too stringent requirements for women to meet, and cultural barriers may further complicate access.

But there is an alternative: Islamic finance, which prohibits interest and promotes risk-sharing, offers an alternative that aligns with the values of many Muslim women.

Microfinance institutions and crowdfunding platforms are also valuable resources for women entrepreneurs. They tend to have more flexible terms and can be a real lifeline for women starting or expanding their businesses. Giving women the information and training to access these financial resources is crucial for giving them a leg up.

Additionally, creating funding programs and grants for women can help level the playing field and encourage more women to pursue entrepreneurship.

Digital Literacy and Technology

In today's digital age, technology is a powerful tool for entrepreneurship. Digital literacy—understanding how to use technology effectively—is essential for modern business operations. This includes social media marketing, e-commerce, data analysis, and cybersecurity.

Tailoring training programs specifically for Muslim women entrepreneurs and focusing on these digital skills can help them unlock the potential of technology for their businesses. Take social media, for instance. Mastering social media platforms like Instagram and TikTok can significantly expand their reach and customer base. E-commerce platforms provide an avenue to sell products globally, breaking down geographic barriers.

Also, offering workshops on digital tools like accounting software, customer relationship management (CRM) systems, and online collaboration tools can streamline business operations and improve efficiency.

Promoting Gender Equality and Economic Empowerment in Muslim Communities

Promoting gender equality and economic empowerment requires a multifaceted approach that involves individuals, communities, and institutions. Creating an environment where women feel supported and valued in their entrepreneurial endeavours is essential.

Cultural and Societal Change

As we've touched upon in this book, cultural norms and societal expectations can sometimes restrict women's participation in business. But here's the thing: we can challenge and change these norms by promoting positive role models and success stories of Muslim women entrepreneurs. By celebrating the achievements of women in business, we can inspire others and shift perceptions about what women can achieve.

And it's not just about individuals stepping up. Community leaders and religious scholars have a significant role to play, too. By advocating for gender equality and economic empowerment and referencing Islamic teachings that support women's rights and contributions, they can help foster a more inclusive and supportive environment. The Quran states,

> "And their Lord responded to them, 'Never will I allow to be lost the work of [any] worker among you, whether male or female; you are of one another'" (Quran 3:195)

This drives home the point that men's and women's contributions are equally valuable.

Public awareness campaigns and educational programs can also help change cultural attitudes. When schools, media, and community organisations team up to promote the importance of gender equality and the benefits of women's economic participation, we're laying the groundwork for profound change. Celebrating International Women's Day and other events is not just about celebrating the contributions of women – it's also about reinforcing positive messages about the value of gender equality.

Policy and Institutional Support

Governments and institutions can play a crucial role in supporting women's entrepreneurship through policies and programs. This includes providing grants and subsidies targeted at women-owned businesses, creating incubator and accelerator programs, and ensuring women have equal access to business development services.

It's not only about the business "stuff". Policies that promote work-life balance, like parental leave and flexible working hours, can also be game-changers for women entrepreneurs who are juggling business and family life. Having legal frameworks in place to protect women's rights in the workplace and in business transactions is absolutely crucial for creating a fair and equitable business environment.

Governments should be investing in research, too. By identifying and addressing the barriers holding women back in entrepreneurship, they can tailor policies that truly meet women's needs and help them thrive.

Community-Based Initiatives

Community-based initiatives can be highly effective in supporting women entrepreneurs. Local business associations, women's groups, and non-profit organisations can offer essential resources like training, mentorship, and networking opportunities. These groups can also advocate for women's rights and work to eliminate barriers to entrepreneurship.

Creating safe spaces where women can openly share their experiences, challenges, and successes fosters a sense of solidarity and collective empowerment. These community initiatives also raise awareness about the importance of women's economic participation and its benefits for the broader community. Organising local markets, fairs, and exhibitions can also provide platforms for women entrepreneurs to showcase their products and services, gaining visibility and attracting customers.

Promoting Entrepreneurship from a Young Age

Instilling an entrepreneurial mindset from a young age can also make a difference in the long run. Schools and educational programs should weave entrepreneurship education into their curricula, teaching students about business basics, financial literacy, and innovative thinking.

It's crucial to encourage young girls to follow their passions and give them the skills and confidence to explore entrepreneurial ventures.

But it doesn't stop there. Extracurricular programs like business clubs and competitions can give children hands-on experience and spark their interest in entrepreneurship as a viable career path.

Also, role models and mentors can make all the difference. They can offer guidance, motivation, and real-life advice to help the next generation of women entrepreneurs thrive.

Plus, offering internships and work experience opportunities in various industries gives young women a chance to dip their toes in the business world and learn valuable insights and skills that'll come in handy when they're ready to start their own entrepreneurial endeavours.

Case Studies of Successful Muslim Women Entrepreneurs

To illustrate the impact of these strategies, let's explore some case studies of successful Muslim women entrepreneurs who have made significant contributions to their fields.

Rana Dajani: Scientist and Social Entrepreneur

Rana Dajani, a Jordanian molecular biologist, is a shining example of how education and entrepreneurship can intersect. In addition to her scientific achievements, Rana founded the "We Love Reading" program, which promotes literacy and education among children in Jordan and beyond. Her initiative has reached thousands of children, empowering them with the gift of reading and knowledge.

Rana's work demonstrates the power of combining scientific expertise with social entrepreneurship. By addressing a critical social need—literacy—she has created a sustainable model that benefits her community and inspires others to take action. The "We Love Reading" program trains local women to read aloud to children, fostering a love for reading and enhancing literacy rates. This initiative not only promotes education but also empowers women by involving them as active participants in community development. Rana's innovative approach has garnered international recognition, illustrating the profound impact that a dedicated individual can have on society.

Dr Haifa Jamal Al-Lail: Academic Leader and Advocate

Dr Haifa Jamal Al-Lail is the president of Effat University in Saudi Arabia, a leading institution for women's education. Under her leadership, Effat University has expanded its programs and increased its impact, providing women with the education and skills needed to succeed in various fields.

Dr Haifa's efforts to promote women's education and empowerment have profoundly impacted her community. By fostering a supportive educational environment, she has enabled countless women to pursue their dreams. Under her tenure, Effat University has introduced innovative programs in fields such as engineering, business, and architecture, programs traditionally dominated by men. Dr Haifa has also championed partnerships with international institutions, bringing global perspectives to her students and enhancing the university's reputation. Her leadership exemplifies how educational institutions can drive social change and economic development by empowering women.

Zainab Salbi: Humanitarian and Founder of Women for Women International

Zainab Salbi, an Iraqi-American humanitarian, founded Women for Women International, an organisation that supports women survivors of war by providing them with the resources and training needed to rebuild their lives. Since its inception, the organisation has helped over 500,000 women across several conflict-affected countries.

Zainab's work highlights the importance of providing holistic support to women in challenging circumstances. Her organisation addresses not only economic empowerment but also social and emotional well-being, creating a comprehensive support system for women in need. Women for Women International offers vocational training, rights awareness, health education, and financial literacy, enabling women to gain independence and rebuild their communities. Zainab's approach demonstrates the power of comprehensive, compassionate support in transforming lives and fostering resilience in the face of adversity.

Conclusion

Empowering Muslim women entrepreneurs today involves a combination of education, support, and the promotion of gender equality. By drawing on Islamic principles and modern best practices, we can create an entrepreneurial ecosystem that supports and celebrates the contributions of Muslim women. Picture this: a world where every woman, regardless of background, can chase her dreams and build something incredible.

The stories of successful Muslim women entrepreneurs, both past and present, serve as powerful reminders of the potential for women to drive economic growth and social change.

As we continue to support and empower Muslim women entrepreneurs, we must also work to challenge and change societal norms and policies that restrict their opportunities. Creating an environment that values and supports women's economic participation can build a more inclusive and prosperous future for all—a world where everyone, regardless of gender or background, has an equal shot at success.

The journey of empowerment is ongoing and requires the collective efforts of individuals, communities, and institutions. By working together, we can ensure that Muslim women entrepreneurs have the tools, resources, and support they need to succeed and thrive in the modern global economy.

Chapter Four

Empowering Muslim Women Through Education and Training

Investing in Women's Education and Skills Development

As discussed in the last chapter, the journey toward empowering Muslim women entrepreneurs lies in education and skills development. Equipping women with knowledge and practical skills cannot be overstated. This chapter explores the critical role of education and training in fostering entrepreneurial spirit and enabling Muslim women to thrive in the business world. By investing in women's education and providing them with the necessary tools, we pave the way for a future where women can contribute meaningfully to the global economy.

The Importance of Education in Islam

Islam values the pursuit of knowledge. The Quran and Hadith emphasise the importance of education for all Muslims, regardless of gender. Prophet Muhammad (pbuh) said,

> "Seeking knowledge is an obligation upon every Muslim" (Sunan Ibn Majah)

This hadith underscores the duty of every Muslim to seek knowledge and personal growth.

The Quran further supports this by highlighting the significance of education and reflection. In Surah Al-Mujadila, it is stated,

> "Allah will raise those who have believed among you and those who were given knowledge, by degrees" (Quran 58:11)

This verse illustrates the elevated status that Allah grants to those who pursue knowledge, reinforcing the idea that education is a means of achieving both personal and societal advancement.

Formal Education: Building a Strong Foundation

Formal education forms the backbone of skills development and empowerment. For Muslim women, access to quality education from primary through higher education is absolutely essential. These educational institutions serve as the bedrock for shaping future entrepreneurs by equipping them with the knowledge and skills necessary to navigate the business world.

1. **Primary and Secondary Education**: A solid foundation in primary and secondary education is vital for developing basic literacy, numeracy, and critical thinking skills. Without a solid foundation, the structure simply can't withstand the test of time. Similarly, without access to quality education, aspiring entrepreneurs may lack the tools and resources to succeed.

Governments and educational organisations must work to eliminate barriers to education for girls. This includes addressing issues such as child marriage, poverty, and cultural norms that may hinder girls' education. By creating a supportive and inclusive educational environment, we can ensure that all girls have the opportunity to reach their full potential.

Efforts to improve access to education must include building more schools in underserved areas, providing scholarships, and offering free or subsidised school supplies. Community outreach programs are essential for changing societal attitudes towards girls' education. By engaging with families and communities, we can emphasise its importance for the development and prosperity of the entire community.

2. **Higher Education**: Higher education provides women with specialised knowledge and skills crucial for entrepreneurship. Universities and colleges offer courses in business administration, finance, marketing, and other fields that are directly applicable to running a successful business. These institutions also double as hubs for innovation and networking, allowing women to connect with mentors, peers, and industry leaders.

Scholarships and financial aid programs specifically tailored for women can significantly enhance access to higher education. Additionally, universities can introduce flexible learning options, such as online courses and part-time programs, to accommodate women balancing family life.

To improve students' opportunities, universities can forge partnerships with industries to provide practical training and internships. This real-world exposure can not only bolster students' employability but equip them with invaluable skills.

Career counselling services can guide women in choosing fields that align with their interests and market needs, paving the way for promising career trajectories.

3. **Vocational Training and Certification Programs**: Vocational training and certification programs provide practical skills that can be immediately applied in the workforce. These programs are particularly valuable for women who may not have the opportunity to pursue traditional higher education. Vocational training can cover a wide range of fields, from IT and healthcare to culinary arts and fashion design.

Collaboration between organisations and governments is key to offering affordable and accessible vocational training programs. By aligning these programs with market needs, we can ensure that women are equipped with in-demand skills, increasing their employability and entrepreneurial potential.

Vocational programs could include business management training and teaching women how to kickstart and manage their own businesses. Workshops on financial literacy, marketing, and customer service can further enhance their entrepreneurial skills.

Providing access to tools and resources, such as microloans and business incubators, can help women turn their vocational training into successful enterprises.

4. **Continuous Professional Development**: Education does not end with formal schooling; continuous professional development is essential for staying competitive in the ever-evolving business landscape. Women entrepreneurs should have access to ongoing training and development opportunities to update their skills and knowledge.

Professional development programs can include advanced courses, seminars, and workshops on the latest industry trends and technologies. Networking events and professional associations can also provide platforms for women to learn from their peers and industry leaders.

Encouraging a culture of lifelong learning helps women stay adaptable and innovative, allowing them to respond effectively to new challenges and opportunities. Companies can support this by offering professional development programs for their employees and fostering a workforce that is skilled, motivated, and ready to take on leadership roles.

Skills Development: Equipping Women for Success

In addition to formal education, skills development is crucial in empowering women entrepreneurs. Practical skills, ranging from financial literacy to digital marketing, are essential for running a successful business. Here, we explore and give an overview of the key areas of skills development that can significantly impact women's entrepreneurial journeys.

1. **Financial Literacy**: For entrepreneurs, this includes budgeting, accounting, financial planning, and understanding financial statements. Financial literacy enables women to make informed business decisions, manage cash flow, and plan for growth.

Workshops and training programs focused on financial literacy can empower women to take control of their business finances. Non-profit organisations, government agencies, and financial institutions can offer these programs. Additionally, providing resources such as financial planning tools and templates can help women apply these skills in their daily operations. Access to financial advisors and one-on-one coaching can also provide personalised guidance, assisting women confidently navigate complex financial decisions. This financial literacy area will be elaborated on further in the chapter.

2. **Digital Skills**: Being tech-savvy is a must in today's digital age. From understanding how to use digital tools and platforms for marketing to e-commerce, digital skills enable women to reach a broader audience, streamline their processes, and compete in the global marketplace.

Training programs focusing on digital literacy, social media marketing, e-commerce, and cybersecurity can help women leverage technology to grow their businesses. Online courses, webinars, and workshops can provide flexible learning opportunities for women to develop these skills. Moreover, digital literacy extends to understanding data analytics, using software for project management, and adopting digital payment systems, which can further enhance operational efficiency and customer satisfaction.

3. **Leadership and Management Skills**: Running a successful business requires effective leadership and management skills. This means leading a team, making strategic decisions, and effectively managing resources. Women can develop these skills through leadership training programs, which nurture confidence and competence in their entrepreneurial roles.

Mentorship programs are also another valuable avenue for honing leadership skills. Experienced mentors provide guidance, share insights, and support women as they navigate the challenges of entrepreneurship. Peer networks and professional associations can also provide opportunities for women to learn from each other and build their leadership capacities. Workshops on conflict resolution, team building, and strategic planning can further hone their leadership abilities, enabling them to inspire and drive their teams towards shared goals.

4. **Communication and Negotiation Skills**: Building relationships, securing deals, and resolving conflicts all hinge on effective communication and negotiation. Women entrepreneurs must articulate their ideas, negotiate terms, and advocate for their businesses with finesse.

Hands-on workshops and training sessions are invaluable for women for honing these critical skills. Through role-playing exercises, case studies, and interactive activities, women gain practical experience and boost their confidence. Additionally, understanding cultural nuances and practising active listening can enhance their ability to engage with diverse stakeholders and forge strong business partnerships.

The Role of Mentorship and Peer Support

Mentorship and peer support are invaluable resources for women entrepreneurs. Access to experienced mentors and a supportive peer network provides guidance, encouragement, and practical advice. These relationships help women navigate the complexities of entrepreneurship and build successful businesses.

1. **Mentorship Programs**: This involves pairing experienced entrepreneurs with aspiring women entrepreneurs. Mentors can offer insights based on their own experiences, goal-setting assistance, and support during challenging times. Effective mentorship programs should match mentors and mentees based on their specific needs and goals, with structured, regular check-ins ensuring accountability and continuous development.

2. **Peer Networks and Support Groups**: Offering a sense of community, shared learning experiences, and mutual support, peer networks connect women entrepreneurs facing similar challenges. Through regular meetings, online forums, and social events, women can learn from each other and build strong connections in the process. These networks can also facilitate knowledge sharing on best practices, market trends, and emerging opportunities, fostering a collaborative environment for growth.

3. **Professional Associations**: Joining professional associations and industry groups can be incredibly valuable for women entrepreneurs. These organisations often provide access to industry-specific training, conferences, and events, allowing women to stay up-to-date about trends and best practices in their fields. Plus, membership in these associations can also enhance credibility and provide a platform for advocacy and influence within their industries.

Promoting Financial Literacy and Entrepreneurial Skills

As we touched upon at the beginning of the chapter, money really matters. Financial literacy and entrepreneurial skills are the bedrock of any successful business venture. For Muslim women entrepreneurs, these competencies are particularly crucial in navigating the complexities of modern markets and achieving sustainable growth. This chapter delves into the importance of financial literacy, practical ways to enhance these skills and the broader impact on women's empowerment and economic development.

The Importance of Financial Literacy

Financial literacy involves understanding and effectively using various financial skills, including personal financial management, budgeting, and investing. For entrepreneurs, it also encompasses the ability to interpret financial statements, manage cash flow, and make informed decisions that affect the financial health of their businesses.

The Quran underscores the importance of careful financial management and honesty in transactions. It states,

> "O you who have believed, do not consume one another's wealth unjustly or send it [in bribery] to the rulers in order that [they might aid] you [to] consume a portion of the wealth of the people in sin, while you know [it is unlawful]" (Quran 2:188)

This verse highlights the necessity of ethical financial conduct, a key component of financial literacy.

For Muslim women, mastering financial literacy isn't just about personal empowerment; it's a broader social responsibility. By managing finances effectively, women can contribute to the economic stability of their families and communities, promote ethical business practices, and drive social change.

Enhancing Financial Literacy

Improving financial literacy among Muslim women entrepreneurs involves several practical steps. These include education and training programs, access to resources, and mentorship.

1. **Education and Training Programs**: Educational institutions, non-profit organisations, and government agencies can design tailored programs to enhance financial literacy. These programs should cover fundamental topics such as budgeting, saving, investing, and understanding credit and address business-specific topics like financial planning, cash flow management, and financial reporting.

Workshops, seminars, and online courses offer flexible learning opportunities that can accommodate women's diverse needs. For instance, online courses allow women to learn at their own pace and on their schedules, making education more accessible for those balancing multiple responsibilities. Moreover, integrating financial literacy into the curriculum of schools and universities ensures young women start developing these crucial skills early in their academic journey.

2. **Access to Resources**: Providing access to financial resources and tools is essential for building financial literacy. This includes access to financial calculators, budgeting templates, and investment guides and providing information on various financial products and services, such as savings accounts, loans, and insurance. Equipped with these tools, women can confidently make informed financial decisions.

Financial institutions can play a pivotal role by offering financial education as part of their services. Banks, for example, can host financial literacy workshops and provide resources tailored to the needs of women entrepreneurs. Partnerships between financial institutions and community organisations can further extend the reach of these resources. Additionally, mobile applications and online platforms that offer financial education and management tools can be highly effective in reaching a wider audience.

3. **Mentorship and Peer Support**: Mentorship and peer support are crucial for reinforcing financial literacy. Experienced mentors can offer practical advice, share their own financial experiences, and guide on complex financial matters. Peer support groups allow women to share their experiences, discuss challenges, and learn from each other.

Developing Entrepreneurial Skills

Developing entrepreneurial skills, including strategic planning, marketing, leadership, and innovation, is essential for business success, along with financial literacy.

1. **Strategic Planning**: Strategic planning involves setting long-term goals, identifying opportunities, and developing action plans to achieve these goals. It requires understanding the market, competitive landscape, and internal strengths and weaknesses. For Muslim women entrepreneurs, strategic planning is crucial for sustainable business growth.

Training programs that focus on strategic planning can help women develop these skills. These programs should include practical exercises, case studies, and interactive sessions that allow participants to apply their knowledge. They can also offer simulation exercises where participants can practice making strategic decisions in a risk-free environment, enhancing their ability to think critically and plan effectively.

Additionally, workshops on market analysis, SWOT (Strengths, Weaknesses, Opportunities, Threats) analysis, and goal-setting can give women the tools they need to create comprehensive business strategies. Encouraging women to develop business plans and regularly review and adjust their strategies can ensure they remain adaptable and prepared for market changes.

2. **Marketing and Branding**: Effective marketing and branding are essential for attracting and retaining customers. This includes understanding target markets, creating compelling value propositions, and developing effective marketing strategies. Digital marketing skills, such as social media marketing, content creation, and search engine optimisation, are particularly important in today's digital age.

Workshops and courses on marketing and branding can equip women with the skills to promote their businesses effectively. These programs could cover traditional marketing techniques and advanced digital marketing strategies. Practical sessions on creating marketing campaigns, using analytics tools to measure performance, and adjusting strategies based on data insights could also be particularly beneficial.

Additionally, providing access to marketing tools and platforms can help women implement their marketing strategies. Partnerships with digital marketing firms and platforms can offer women entrepreneurs discounted access to professional marketing services and tools, further enhancing their marketing capabilities.

3. **Leadership and Management**: Leadership and management skills are critical for guiding a business, involving decision-making, problem-solving, communication, and team management. Strong leadership inspires employees, fosters positivity, and drives business growth.

Women can develop these skills through training programs and mentorship, covering conflict resolution, effective communication, delegation, and performance management. Role-playing scenarios and leadership simulations could also provide women with hands-on experience managing teams and making strategic decisions.

Encouraging women to take on leadership roles boosts confidence and experience. Participating in leadership workshops and networking events facilitates learning from successful leaders and diverse strategies.

4. **Innovation and Creativity**: Innovation and creativity are key drivers of business success. This involves developing new products or services, improving existing processes, and finding innovative solutions to business challenges. Cultivating a culture of innovation can help businesses stay competitive and adapt to changing market conditions.

Initiatives promoting innovation feature workshops in design thinking, brainstorming sessions, and innovation labs. These programs teach techniques for generating creative ideas, evaluating potential solutions, and implementing innovative changes.

Allowing women to collaborate and share ideas can also stimulate creativity and innovation. Creating innovation hubs or co-working spaces where women can work together, share resources, and brainstorm solutions can foster a supportive environment for creative thinking and problem-solving.

The Impact of Financial Literacy and Entrepreneurial Skills on Women's Empowerment

When women are equipped with financial literacy and entrepreneurial skills, it not only empowers them individually but also contributes to broader economic development. Here's how:

1. **Economic Independence**: Financial literacy and entrepreneurial skills empower women to generate income, build wealth, and support their families. With better financial management skills, women can become more financially independent and invest in their children's education, healthcare, and overall well-being while also contributing to the upliftment of future generations.

2. **Confidence and Self-Esteem**: Knowledge and skills build confidence and self-esteem. Women who are financially literate and skilled

in entrepreneurship are more likely to pursue business opportunities, take calculated risks, and overcome challenges. This confidence can translate into greater success and satisfaction in their personal and professional lives. Moreover, confident women are more likely to mentor others, creating a ripple effect of empowerment within their communities.

3. **Social and Economic Impact**: Empowered women entrepreneurs can drive social and economic change. By creating jobs, supporting local economies, and promoting ethical business practices, they contribute to the overall development of their communities. Successful women entrepreneurs can be role models, inspiring others to pursue their entrepreneurial dreams. They can also advocate for policies that support women's entrepreneurship, contributing to systemic changes that benefit all women.

4. **Promotion of Ethical Practices**: Financial literacy and entrepreneurial skills aligned with Islamic principles promote ethical business practices. Muslim women entrepreneurs knowledgeable about finance and business ethics are better equipped to conduct their businesses in a manner that aligns with their faith and values. This includes fair dealing, honesty, and social responsibility.

Prophet Muhammad (pbuh) emphasised the importance of ethical business conduct. He said,

> "The truthful and trustworthy merchant is with the Prophets, the truthful, and the martyrs" (Al-Tirmidhi)

This hadith highlights the high regard for honesty and integrity in business. Women entrepreneurs who adhere to these principles can build trust with their customers, employees, and partners, fostering long-term business relationships and a positive reputation.

Case Studies of Successful Muslim Women Entrepreneurs

To illustrate the impact of financial literacy and entrepreneurial skills, let's explore some case studies of successful Muslim women entrepreneurs who have leveraged these competencies to achieve remarkable success.

Iman Aldebe: Fashion Designer and Entrepreneur

Iman Aldebe is a Swedish-Jordanian fashion designer known for her innovative hijab designs. Her brand, Iman Aldebe, combines traditional Islamic attire with modern fashion trends, appealing to a global audience. Iman's success can be attributed to her strong financial acumen, creative marketing strategies, and commitment to quality.

Iman's journey began with a passion for fashion and a desire to create stylish and comfortable hijabs. She invested time learning about the fashion industry, financial management, and digital marketing. Her ability to blend creativity with business skills has enabled her to build a successful brand that resonates with Muslim women around the world.

Initially, Iman faced challenges entering a market with limited understanding and appreciation for contemporary Islamic fashion. However, through strategic market research and a deep understanding of her customer base, she crafted designs that met the needs and preferences of modern Muslim women. Her savvy use of social media platforms for marketing and customer engagement significantly expanded her brand's reach.

Iman's financial literacy helped her make informed decisions about pricing, sourcing materials, and managing her brand's growth. By maintaining high ethical standards in her business practices, she gained the trust and loyalty of her customers, ensuring long-term success. Today, Iman Aldebe's designs are featured in major fashion shows and retail stores worldwide, symbolising the fusion of tradition and modernity.

Dr Hayat Sindi: Scientist and Entrepreneur

Dr Hayat Sindi, a Saudi Arabian scientist and entrepreneur, co-founded Diagnostics For All, a non-profit organisation developing affordable diagnostic tools for developing countries. Her work combines scientific innovation with entrepreneurial skills to address global health challenges.

Dr Sindi's success is rooted in her strong educational background, financial literacy, and leadership skills. She secured funding from various sources, managed complex projects, and led her team with vision and determination. Her pioneering work in science and social entrepreneurship has earned her numerous accolades and recognition.

On top of her scientific prowess, Dr Sindi's entrepreneurial spirit has driven her to explore innovative funding models, including grants, partnerships, and social impact investments. She has adeptly navigated the complexities of non-profit management, ensuring that Diagnostics For All can deliver on its mission to provide accessible healthcare solutions.

Dr Sindi's leadership style is characterised by her ability to inspire and mobilise her team, fostering a collaborative environment where scientific and entrepreneurial talents can flourish. Her dedication to social impact extends beyond her organisation; she actively mentors young women in STEM fields, encouraging them to pursue careers in science and entrepreneurship.

Farah Mohamed: Social Entrepreneur and Advocate

Farah Mohamed, a Canadian-Muslim social entrepreneur, founded G(irls)20, an organisation that empowers young women to become leaders and change-makers. Farah's work focuses on providing training, mentorship, and resources to young women from around the world.

Her strategic planning, fundraising skills, and commitment to social impact drive Farah's success. She has developed partnerships with governments, corporations, and non-profits to support her organisation's mission. Farah's ability to combine entrepreneurial skills with a passion for social justice has made G(irls)20 a powerful force for change.

Under Farah's leadership, G(irls)20 has organised numerous global summits, bringing together young women leaders to discuss and devise solutions to pressing global issues. These summits not only provide participants with valuable leadership training but amplify their voices on international platforms.

Farah's strategic use of media and storytelling has helped raise awareness about gender equality and the importance of women's leadership. Her effective fundraising strategies have secured significant financial support from diverse sources, enabling G(irls)20 to expand its programs and reach more young women globally.

The Broader Impact of These Entrepreneurs

These case studies highlight the broader impact of financial literacy and entrepreneurial skills on women's empowerment and economic development. Each of these women has not only achieved personal success but has also contributed significantly to their communities and beyond.

Economic Growth and Job Creation: These entrepreneurs have created job opportunities and stimulated economic activity within their respective industries. Iman Aldebe's fashion brand, for instance, has created jobs in design, manufacturing, marketing, and retail, contributing to the economic growth of the fashion industry.

Social Impact and Community Development: Through their ventures, these women have addressed critical social issues and contributed to community development. Dr Hayat Sindi's work in affordable diagnostics has had a profound impact on healthcare accessibility in developing countries, while Farah Mohamed's G(irls)20 has empowered young women globally, fostering the next generation of leaders and change-makers.

Role Models and Inspiration: These successful entrepreneurs serve as role models, demonstrating that women can overcome barriers and achieve great success with the right skills and determination. They inspire other women to pursue their entrepreneurial dreams, creating a ripple effect of empowerment.

Promotion of Ethical and Sustainable Practices: By aligning their businesses with ethical principles, these women have promoted sustainable and responsible business practices. Their commitment to quality, integrity, and social responsibility sets a standard for other entrepreneurs to follow.

The stories of Iman Aldebe, Dr Hayat Sindi, and Farah Mohamed exemplify the transformative power of financial literacy and entrepreneurial skills. These women have leveraged their knowledge and skills to build successful enterprises that not only achieve financial success but also drive social change and community development. Their journeys underscore the importance of empowering more women with the tools and resources needed to succeed in entrepreneurship. By doing so, we can foster a more inclusive and prosperous future where women play a pivotal role in shaping the global economy.

Conclusion

Promoting financial literacy and entrepreneurial skills is essential for empowering Muslim women entrepreneurs. By providing education, resources, and support, we can equip women with the tools they need to succeed in business and achieve economic independence. The principles of Islam emphasise the importance of knowledge, ethical conduct, and social responsibility, offering a solid foundation for women to build upon.

As we continue to support and empower Muslim women entrepreneurs, we must also work to challenge and change societal norms and policies that restrict their opportunities. Creating an environment that values and supports women's economic participation can build a more inclusive and prosperous future for all.

The journey of empowerment is ongoing and requires the collective efforts of individuals, communities, and institutions. By working together, we can ensure that Muslim women entrepreneurs have the tools, resources, and support they need to succeed and thrive in the modern global economy with confidence.

Chapter Five

Breaking Barriers: Overcoming Challenges in Business

Addressing Cultural and Societal Constraints

Starting and growing a business can be a challenging endeavour for anyone, but for Muslim women, there can be additional cultural and societal barriers to navigate. These constraints often stem from deeply ingrained social norms, gender biases, and sometimes even misinterpretations of religious teachings. This chapter explores strategies for overcoming these barriers, advocating for gender equality, and promoting women's rights in business. By addressing these challenges head-on, Muslim women entrepreneurs can pave the way for a more inclusive and supportive business environment.

Understanding Cultural and Societal Constraints

Cultural and societal constraints are deeply embedded in the social fabric and often influence the roles and expectations of women. These constraints can manifest in various forms, including limited access to education, restrictions on mobility, and societal pressures to prioritise family responsibilities over professional ambitions.

Gender Roles and Expectations

In many cultures, there exists the traditional gender role construct that women should handle domestic duties while men are expected to be the breadwinners. This division of roles can limit women's opportunities to pursue education and careers. The Quran, however, encourages both men and women to seek knowledge and contribute to society. It states,

> "And whoever does righteous deeds, whether male or female, while being a believer – those will enter Paradise" (Quran 4:124)

This verse clarifies that both men and women are equally capable of achieving righteousness and success.

These traditional expectations can create conflict for women who aspire to professional achievements. Juggling family obligations with career aspirations often demands support from family members and society. Plus, societal expectations can lead to internalised beliefs that hinder women's self-confidence and aspirations.

Limited Access to Education

Access to education should be a given, yet many girls and women around the world are still denied this opportunity due to cultural and societal norms. Education isn't just important for personal growth; it's crucial for developing the skills and knowledge needed for entrepreneurship. Prophet Muhammad (pbuh) said,

> "Seeking knowledge is an obligation upon every Muslim" (Sunan Ibn Majah).

This hadith underscores the importance of education for all Muslims, regardless of gender.

In regions where education for girls is not prioritised, women face significant barriers to acquiring the basic literacy and numeracy skills necessary for business. Lack of education limits their ability to understand and engage with the market, manage finances, and leverage technology effectively. Without these foundational skills, women's economic participation remains significantly hindered.

Mobility and Social Restrictions

In some cultures, women's mobility is restricted due to safety concerns or societal norms. This can limit their ability to attend school, work, or participate in community activities, hindering their entrepreneurial aspirations. Addressing these barriers requires a collective effort to create safe and supportive environments for them.

When women are restricted from moving around freely, it's not only about missing school or work—it can prevent them from accessing markets, attending business meetings, or engaging in networking opportunities that are crucial for business development. These limitations can isolate women from the broader economic and social networks that are essential for business success. That's why it's crucial to create more inclusive environments that support women's mobility and promote their chances of success.

Strategies for Overcoming Cultural and Societal Constraints

Empowering Muslim women entrepreneurs requires us to devise strategies for tackling and overcoming cultural and societal barriers. This involves a combination of education, advocacy, and community support.

Promoting Positive Role Models

As already mentioned in this book, elevating successful Muslim women entrepreneurs as role models can inspire others to pursue their entrepreneurial dreams. These role models can demonstrate that balancing cultural and religious values with professional success is possible. For example, Khadijah bint Khuwaylid, the first wife of Prophet Muhammad (pbuh), was a successful businesswoman whose achievements continue to inspire women today.

Role models can share their stories through media, public speaking, and mentorship programs, providing tangible examples of success. Showcasing their journeys can help challenge stereotypes and encourage other women facing similar challenges.

Education and Awareness Campaigns

Raising awareness about the importance of women's education and economic participation is crucial. Education campaigns can challenge traditional gender roles and highlight the benefits of empowering women. These campaigns should involve community leaders, religious scholars, and the media to ensure a broad reach and impact.

Public awareness campaigns can include workshops, seminars, and community discussions that educate both men and women about the value of women's contributions to the economy. Highlighting success stories and the positive outcomes of women's economic participation can help shift public perception and promote gender equality.

Community Support and Advocacy

Building community support for women's entrepreneurship involves getting everyone on board, from community leaders to families and religious institutions. Advocacy efforts can focus on promoting gender equality and addressing misconceptions about women's roles in society. With a supportive community environment, women feel more empowered to pursue their business goals.

Community programs can involve family members in discussions about gender roles, pushing for fairer sharing of domestic responsibilities. Religious leaders also have a big role to play, interpreting religious texts in ways that back women's empowerment and economic participation.

Legal and Policy Reforms

Advocating for legal and policy reforms that promote gender equality is essential for creating an enabling environment for women entrepreneurs. This means implementing laws that protect women's rights, guarantee equal access to education and employment, and promote a healthy work-life balance. Governments and policymakers play a critical role in driving these reforms.

Policies like providing childcare support, parental leave, and flexible working hours can help women balance work and family responsibilities. Moreover, legal reforms that protect women from discrimination and violence are equally as essential for ensuring their safe and equitable participation in the workforce.

Providing Safe Spaces and Networks

Creating safe spaces where women can learn, network, and collaborate is vital for their professional development. Whether it's women's business associations, networking groups, or coworking spots, these spaces provide the support and resources women need to thrive. Plus, these spaces are perfect platforms for advocacy and community building.

In these safe spaces, women can share experiences, access mentorship, and receive training in a supportive environment. Networking events and business incubators specifically designed for women can help them build connections and access resources essential for business growth.

Case Studies: Overcoming Cultural and Societal Barriers

To illustrate the strategies discussed, let's explore some case studies of Muslim women entrepreneurs who have successfully navigated cultural and societal constraints. These stories showcase the transformative power of education, mentorship, community support, and advocacy in breaking down barriers.

Dr Hayat Sindi: Breaking Barriers in Science and Technology

Dr Hayat Sindi, a Saudi Arabian scientist and entrepreneur, faced significant cultural barriers in her pursuit of a career in science. Despite the challenges, she persevered and became the first woman from the Gulf region to earn a Ph.D. in biotechnology. Dr Sindi co-founded Diagnostics For All, a non-profit organisation developing low-cost diagnostic tools for developing countries.

Dr Sindi's success can be attributed to her determination, education access, and mentor support. From an early age, she showed a strong interest in science, which her family nurtured. She faced societal expectations that often discouraged women from pursuing careers in STEM (Science, Technology, Engineering, and Mathematics) fields. However, her passion for science and the support of her mentors and family helped her to overcome these obstacles.

In her professional journey, Dr Sindi has emphasised the importance of mentorship and community support. She actively mentors young women, encouraging them to pursue their interests in science and technology. Her achievements highlight the critical role that education and mentorship play in breaking down cultural barriers. By serving as a role model, Dr Sindi inspires young women to pursue careers in STEM fields, demonstrating that it's possible to overcome societal constraints and achieve remarkable success with the right support.

Amani Al-Khatahtbeh: Empowering Women Through Media

Amani Al-Khatahtbeh, the founder of MuslimGirl.com, has used media to challenge stereotypes and empower Muslim women. Growing up in the United States, Amani faced cultural and societal pressures that often marginalised Muslim women. She created MuslimGirl.com to provide a platform for Muslim women to share their stories, experiences, and perspectives.

Amani's work has garnered international recognition and has provided a voice for Muslim women in the media. By leveraging digital platforms, she has reached a global audience and advocated for gender equality and women's rights. Through her platform, Amani addresses issues such as Islamophobia, gender discrimination, and cultural stereotypes, empowering Muslim women to speak out and share their narratives.

Her success demonstrates the power of media and technology in overcoming societal constraints. Amani has not only provided a space for Muslim women to express themselves but has also educated a broader audience about the diverse experiences of Muslim women. Her work highlights the importance of digital literacy and the potential of technology to drive social change. By creating and leading MuslimGirl.com, Amani has shown that digital platforms can be powerful tools for advocacy and empowerment.

Muna AbuSulayman: Advocate for Women's Rights and Education

Muna AbuSulayman, a prominent Saudi Arabian media personality and philanthropist, has dedicated her career to advocating for women's rights and education. As the former Executive Director of the Alwaleed Bin Talal Foundation, she has led numerous initiatives to support women's empowerment and social development.

Muna's advocacy efforts have focused on challenging traditional gender roles and promoting education for women. Through her work, she has influenced policy changes and created opportunities for women to pursue their professional aspirations. Her leadership in media and philanthropy has made her a prominent figure in advocating for women's rights in the Middle East.

She has used her platform to raise awareness about the importance of women's education and economic participation. Muna has been instrumental in promoting policies that support women's rights and gender equality. Her efforts have contributed to significant advancements in women's education and empowerment in Saudi Arabia.

Muna's leadership and advocacy demonstrate the impact of policy reforms and community engagement in addressing cultural barriers. By working with policymakers, community leaders, and international organisations, she has helped create an environment that supports women's advancement. Her work underscores the importance of legal and policy reforms in creating a more equitable society for women.

The Role of Islamic Teachings in Empowering Women

Islamic teachings provide a robust framework for advocating for women's rights and empowerment. The Quran and Hadith emphasise justice, equality, and the pursuit of knowledge for both men and women, offering a foundation that supports women's advancement and empowerment in various aspects of life.

Equality and Justice

The Quran emphasises the equality of men and women in their spiritual and social responsibilities. It states,

> "And their Lord responded to them, 'Never will I allow to be lost the work of [any] worker among you, whether male or female; you are of one another'" (Quran 3:195)

This verse highlights the equal value of men's and women's contributions and affirms that both genders are rewarded equally for their deeds.

Prophet Muhammad (pbuh) also emphasised justice and fairness in all aspects of life. He said,

> "All people are equal, as equal as the teeth of a comb. No Arab has any superiority over a non-Arab, nor does a white man have any superiority over a black man, nor does a black man have any superiority over a white man, except by piety and good action" (Musnad Ahmad)

This hadith underscores the principle of equality and the importance of judging individuals based on their actions and character, not their gender or ethnicity.

The Pursuit of Knowledge

Islam encourages all believers to pursue knowledge. Prophet Muhammad (pbuh) said,

> "Seeking knowledge is an obligation upon every Muslim" (Sunan Ibn Majah)

This directive applies to both men and women, emphasising the importance of education for personal and societal development.

Education is a means of empowerment and a tool for achieving justice and equality. By promoting education for women, we align with Islamic teachings and contribute to the overall progress of society. Educated women are better equipped to contribute to economic development, engage in informed decision-making, and raise well-rounded, educated children.

Economic Participation

Islam acknowledges and supports women's right to engage in economic activities and own property. Khadijah bint Khuwaylid, the first wife of Prophet Muhammad (pbuh), is a great example of this. She was a successful businesswoman who managed her own wealth and trade caravans. Her story clearly demonstrates that women have the right to participate in business and contribute to economic development.

The Quran supports this notion by stating,

> "For men is a share of what they have earned, and for women is a share of what they have earned" (Quran 4:32)

This verse underscores the principle of economic justice and the right of women to benefit from their work. Women's financial independence and economic contribution are integral to a balanced and prosperous society.

Practical Steps for Muslim Women Entrepreneurs

If you're a Muslim women entrepreneur and struggling to overcome cultural and societal constraints to achieve success in your business, take inspiration from Khadijah bint Khuwaylid and follow these valuable tips:

1. **Build a Strong Support Network**: Building a strong support network is essential for navigating challenges and achieving success. This network can include your family, friends, mentors, and professional associations. Engaging with like-minded individuals and organisations can provide valuable support, advice, and resources.

Networking with other entrepreneurs, joining business associations, and participating in community groups can open doors to new opportunities and collaborations. Plus, having support networks can give you emotional encouragement and practical help, such as childcare support or business advice.

2. **Pursue Continuous Learning**: Continuous learning is crucial for your personal and professional growth. As a Muslim women entrepreneur, it's important to seek out opportunities for education and training, stay informed about industry trends, and continuously improve your skills. Online courses, workshops, and conferences are great for flexible learning.

Keeping up with the latest technological advancements, market trends, and business strategies will help you stay competitive and innovative. Continuously learning throughout your life nurtures your ability to adapt and bounce back, empowering you to pivot and grow your business in response to changing market conditions.

3. **Advocate for Change**: As a Muslim women entrepreneur, you have the power to actively advocate for change within your community. You can do this by sharing your story, raising awareness about women's rights, and engaging with community leaders. You have the power to challenge and change societal norms!

Through public speaking, writing articles, and participating in panel discussions, you have the opportunity to amplify your voices and influence public opinion. Also, collaborating with NGOs and advocacy groups enables you to empower women and promote social justice.

4. **Leverage Technology**: Harnessing technology opens up a world of possibilities for overcoming societal constraints and expanding business opportunities. By leveraging digital platforms such as e-commerce, social media, and online marketplaces for marketing and networking, you can reach a wider audience and create new business opportunities.

Integrating digital tools into your business can streamline operations, improve efficiency, and reduce costs. From project management software to accounting tools and customer relationship management

(CRM) systems, these technologies can not only enhance productivity but also professionalise your business practices.

5. **Embrace Resilience and Perseverance**: Resilience and perseverance are key qualities for overcoming challenges and achieving success. As a Muslim women entrepreneur, you must stay steadfast on your goals, remain adaptable in the face of challenges, and persist despite setbacks. Draw strength from your faith and the examples of successful women who have come before.

Setting realistic goals, celebrating small victories, and maintaining a positive outlook are important strategies for staying resilient. Being surrounded by a supportive network and mentors will give you the encouragement and advice you need to navigate difficult times and the perseverance to keep going.

Conclusion

Addressing cultural and societal constraints is essential for empowering Muslim women entrepreneurs. By promoting positive role models, raising awareness, building community support, advocating for legal reforms, and creating safe spaces, we can overcome these barriers and create an inclusive environment that supports women's economic participation.

Islamic teachings provide a strong foundation for advocating for gender equality and women's rights. When we sync our efforts with these principles, we promote justice, equality, and the pursuit of knowledge for all.

But this journey of empowerment is ongoing. It's not a sprint; it's a marathon that requires the collective efforts of individuals, communities, and institutions. By working together, we can ensure that Muslim women entrepreneurs have the tools, resources, and support they need not just to survive but thrive in today's modern global economy. Through education, advocacy, and leveraging technology, we can create a more equitable and prosperous future for all.

Navigating Family and Work-Life Balance

Balancing the demands of family life and entrepreneurial ambitions is a challenge faced by many, and for Muslim women, these challenges can be uniquely complex. Yet, with the right strategies and support systems, it's entirely possible to create a fulfilling and successful balance between work and family. This chapter explores practical approaches and supportive policies that can help Muslim women entrepreneurs navigate family responsibilities while pursuing their business dreams.

The Importance of Family in Islam

In Islam, the family is regarded as the cornerstone of society. The Quran emphasises the significance of family life, mutual respect, and support. It states,

> "And We have enjoined upon man, to his parents, good treatment" (Quran 46:15)

This verse highlights the importance of caring for one's family, a value deeply ingrained in Muslim culture.

Prophet Muhammad (pbuh) exemplified the balance between family and responsibilities. He said,

> "The best of you are those who are best to their families, and I am the best among you to my family" (Sunan Ibn Majah)

This hadith underscores the importance of treating the family with kindness and prioritising their well-being. The teachings of Prophet

Muhammad (pbuh) stress the importance of fulfilling familial obligations while pursuing personal and professional goals.

Family life in Islam is built on the principles of mutual respect, compassion, and support. The Quran encourages believers to maintain strong family ties and to honour their parents and elders. It states,

> "And your Lord has decreed that you not worship except Him, and to parents, good treatment" (Quran 17:23)

This verse not only emphasises the importance of worship but also places great importance on the treatment of parents, reflecting the integral role of the family in Islamic teachings.

Challenges of Balancing Family and Work

For many Muslim women entrepreneurs, the dual responsibilities of managing a business and caring for a family can be overwhelming. These challenges often include time management, societal expectations, and the need for supportive networks.

Time Management

Effective time management is crucial for balancing family and work. The demands of running a business can be all-consuming, making it difficult to allocate sufficient time for family responsibilities. If not managed properly, this can lead to stress and burnout. Implementing effective time management strategies, such as setting clear boundaries, prioritising tasks, and creating a structured schedule, can help balance these demands. Time management tools and apps can also assist in organising tasks and setting reminders for important family and business commitments.

Societal Expectations

Societal expectations and traditional gender roles can add pressure on women to prioritise family over career. In many cultures, women are expected to be the primary caregivers, which can limit their opportunities to pursue entrepreneurial ambitions. Overcoming these expectations requires a cultural shift and family and community support. By educating and raising awareness about the capabilities and rights of women, communities can help create an environment where women are encouraged to pursue their entrepreneurial goals. Highlighting successful role models who have balanced family and business can also inspire and motivate others.

Lack of Supportive Networks

A lack of supportive networks, including family, friends, and professional mentors, can make it challenging for women to balance work and family life. Supportive networks are essential for providing practical assistance, emotional support, and guidance. Building a strong support system involves reaching out to like-minded individuals, joining professional organisations, and participating in community groups. These networks can offer valuable resources, such as mentorship programs, networking events, and peer support groups, which can help women navigate the complexities of balancing family and work.

Strategies for Balancing Family and Work

To successfully balance family and work, Muslim women entrepreneurs can adopt several practical strategies. These strategies involve effective time management, seeking support, setting boundaries, and leveraging technology. Perhaps you're a Muslim women entrepreneur struggling to juggle family and work right now. Here are some insightful tips:

Effective Time Management

Managing your time well is essential for balancing multiple responsibilities. Creating a structured schedule that allocates specific times for your work and family can make a big difference. Tools like calendars, planners, and time-tracking apps can help organise daily activities and ensure nothing slips through the cracks.

But it's also equally important to prioritise. Identifying the most important tasks for your business and family can help you manage your time more effectively. Remember, it's important to recognise that it's not always possible to do everything, and sometimes, delegating tasks or saying no is necessary.

Using tools Eisenhower Matrix can help you distinguish between urgent and important tasks, thus ensuring that time is allocated to what truly matters. Also, batch processing similar tasks together can also enhance productivity and help you stay focused, reducing the cognitive load of constantly switching between different types of activities.

Seeking Support

Building a strong support network is vital for managing the demands of family and work. Your network can include family members, friends, mentors, and professional associations. Seeking support from family members for household responsibilities can take some weight off your shoulders. Being open with family about work commitments and seeking their understanding and cooperation is key. Delegating household chores and responsibilities to other family members can create a more balanced environment where everyone pitches in and lightens the load.

Building professional networks and finding mentorship can be a real game-changer. Connecting with other female entrepreneurs with similar challenges can offer practical solutions and emotional support. Mentorship programs are also valuable in getting guidance on how to navigate the complexities of balancing family and work. Joining women's business associations or local entrepreneurial groups can connect you with like-minded individuals who know where you come from – they can offer encouragement, cheer you on, and share their own strategies for success.

Setting Boundaries

Setting clear boundaries between work and family life is important to ensure that neither is neglected. This might mean establishing specific work hours and creating a dedicated workspace at home to minimise distractions. Communicating these boundaries to your family and clients can help manage expectations and help everyone understand when you're off the clock and in work mode.

It's also important to establish boundaries for technology use. In today's digital age, it's easy for work to spill over into personal time through emails and phone calls. Setting boundaries for when to disconnect from work-related communications can help maintain a healthy work-life balance. Implementing "tech-free" zones or times – such as during family meals or before bedtime – can foster more meaningful interactions and prevent burnout. Using features like "Do Not Disturb" mode on your phone can help you stay focused on family time without getting side-tracked by work.

Leveraging Technology

Technology can be a powerful tool for managing work and family responsibilities. Digital tools like project management software, communication apps, and online collaboration platforms can streamline business operations and improve efficiency. These tools can help manage tasks remotely and reduce the time spent on administrative activities. For example, tools like Trello or Asana are great for keeping your projects organised. At the same time, communication apps like Slack or Microsoft Teams facilitate seamless interaction with your team, no matter where they are.

E-commerce platforms and social media should also not be overlooked – they're secret weapons for reaching a wider audience without leaving your house. This can save time and resources, allowing for more flexibility in managing your business and family. Platforms like Shopify or Etsy enable women entrepreneurs to sell products online, while social media tools like Instagram or Facebook are perfect for marketing and customer engagement.

Automating repetitive tasks, such as social media posts or email newsletters, can also free up time for family and other important activities.

Plus, cloud-based storage solutions like Google Drive or Dropbox allow you to access important documents and files from anywhere, enhancing productivity and collaboration.

Self-Care and Wellness Practices

Incorporating self-care and wellness practices into your daily routine is crucial for maintaining physical and mental health. Regular exercise, meditation, and mindfulness activities can work wonders in reducing stress and boosting your overall well-being. Scheduling regular breaks and ensuring adequate rest can prevent burnout and enhance productivity.

Practising gratitude and positive thinking can also build your emotional resilience, making it easier to handle the ups and downs of balancing family and work. So make sure to carve out some time each day for self-care – it's an investment in your health and happiness.

Flexibility and Adaptability

Staying flexible and adaptable are key qualities for managing the dynamic demands of family and entrepreneurship. Being open to adjusting schedules and plans in response to changing circumstances can help you keep that delicate balance in check. For instance, having flexible work hours or the option to work remotely can make it easier to meet family needs without compromising business goals.

Also, developing contingency plans and being prepared for unexpected situations can also provide a sense of control and readiness.

Continuous Learning and Improvement

Never stop learning and growing – it's the secret to staying ahead as a female entrepreneur. Stay updated with your industry's latest trends and best practices by attending workshops, webinars, and conferences. Don't be shy about requesting feedback from mentors, peers, and customers – they can offer valuable perspectives for growth and improvement.

Embracing a mindset of lifelong learning can foster innovation and adaptability, which are essential for long-term success.

Inspirational Stories of Women Balancing Family and Work

To illustrate the strategies and tips discussed, let's explore some inspirational stories of Muslim women who have successfully balanced family and work.

Dr Rimla Akhtar: Sports Administrator and Advocate

Dr Rimla Akhtar is a British sports administrator and advocate who has successfully balanced her career with her family responsibilities. As one of the few Muslim women in sports administration, Dr Akhtar has faced numerous challenges but has managed to excel in her field while maintaining a strong family life.

Dr Akhtar credits her success to effective time management, supportive networks, and clear boundaries. She has utilised flexible work arrangements to manage her responsibilities and has been a vocal advocate for gender equality and diversity in sports. Her story highlights the importance of resilience, support, and advocacy in achieving work-life balance.

Dr Akhtar's journey began with a passion for sports and a determination to break through the barriers that often limit women's participation in this field. She pursued her education rigorously, earning advanced degrees while dedicating time to her family. Dr Akhtar often speaks about the importance of a supportive partner and family who understand and encourage her professional aspirations. Her advocacy work extends beyond her personal career, as she actively mentors young women and champions policies that promote inclusivity and equality in sports administration. Her story is a testament to the impact of community and organisational support in helping women achieve their full potential.

Fadumo Dayib: Politician and Activist

Fadumo Dayib, a Somali politician and activist, has made significant strides in her career while raising her children. As the first woman to run for president in Somalia, Fadumo has faced immense societal pressures and challenges. Despite this, she has managed to balance her political career with her family responsibilities through careful planning, prioritisation, and seeking support from her family and community.

Fadumo's journey emphasises the importance of pursuing one's ambitions while staying grounded in family values. Her story inspires many women who strive to make a difference in their communities while caring for their families. Fadumo's political career is marked by her advocacy for women's rights, education, and healthcare. She often speaks about her children's role in motivating her to create a better future for the next generation. By involving her family in her political activities and seeking their support, Fadumo has been able to navigate the complex demands of her career and personal life. Her resilience in the face of societal expectations and her commitment to her community highlight the power of determination and the importance of a strong support network.

Dina Toki-O: Fashion Designer and Influencer

Dina Toki-O is a British-Egyptian fashion designer and social media influencer who has successfully balanced her career with motherhood. Through her creative designs and engaging online presence, Dina has built a successful brand. As a mother, she has navigated the challenges of raising her children while managing her business.

Dina's success can be attributed to her use of technology, effective time management, and supportive family. By leveraging social media and e-commerce platforms, she has grown her business while maintaining a flexible schedule that allows her to spend quality time with her children. Her ability to connect with her audience through relatable content and transparent sharing of her journey as a working mother has earned her a loyal following. She frequently discusses the importance of self-care and setting realistic goals to avoid burnout. Dina has kept a clear boundary between work and family time by creating a home office and setting designated work hours. Her story underscores the significance of adapting technology to one's advantage and the role of family in providing the necessary support for entrepreneurial success.

Conclusion

Balancing family and work is a multifaceted challenge that requires careful planning, support, and resilience. For Muslim women entrepreneurs, addressing cultural and societal constraints is essential for achieving this balance. Women can successfully navigate their dual responsibilities by adopting effective time management strategies, seeking support, setting boundaries, and leveraging technology.

Supportive policies and initiatives at the organisational and governmental levels can further enhance the ability of women to balance family and work. Flexible work arrangements, comprehensive parental leave policies, childcare support, and training programs are crucial for creating an enabling environment.

As we continue to support and empower Muslim women entrepreneurs, fostering a culture of balance and support is important. By working together, we can create an environment where women can thrive in their professional and personal lives, contributing to society's overall progress and prosperity.

Chapter Six

Leadership Development and Skills Enhancement

Building Leadership Skills Among Muslim Women Entrepreneurs

Leadership is a critical component of entrepreneurial success. For Muslim women entrepreneurs, developing strong leadership skills is essential for navigating the challenges of business, inspiring teams, and achieving sustainable growth. This chapter explores the importance of leadership development, provides practical strategies for building effective leadership skills, and highlights the unique perspectives and strengths that Muslim women bring to leadership roles.

The Importance of Leadership Development

Leadership development is more than just acquiring managerial skills; it involves cultivating a mindset of continuous improvement, ethical decision-making, and inspiring and guiding others. The Quran encourages the pursuit of excellence and the development of personal qualities fundamental to effective leadership. It states,

"And those who strive for Us - We will surely guide them to Our ways. And indeed, Allah is with the doers of good" (Quran 29:69)

This verse underscores the importance of striving for excellence and seeking guidance in all endeavours, including leadership.

Prophet Muhammad (pbuh) exemplified the qualities of a great leader through his actions and teachings. He emphasised the importance of justice, compassion, humility, and integrity. In one hadith, he said,

"The leader of a people is their servant" (Sunan Ibn Majah)

This highlights the concept of servant leadership, where the leader prioritises the well-being and development of their followers.

Key Leadership Skills for Muslim Women Entrepreneurs

To be effective leaders, Muslim women entrepreneurs need to develop a range of skills that enable them to manage their businesses, inspire their teams, and navigate the complexities of the business world. These skills include effective communication, strategic thinking, decision-making, and emotional intelligence.

If you're a Muslim female entrepreneur wanting to improve your leadership skills, the following tips will be helpful to you:

1. Effective Communication

Effective communication is the cornerstone of successful leadership. It means conveying ideas clearly, listening actively, and engaging in meaningful dialogue with team members, customers, and stakeholders. Good communication fosters trust, resolves conflicts, and enhances collaboration.

Practical strategies for improving communication skills include:

- **Active Listening**: Paying close attention to what others say, asking clarifying questions, and providing feedback. This not only shows respect but also builds trust and stronger relationships. When people feel heard and valued, they're happier and more productive.

- **Clear and Concise Messaging**: Being clear and concise in verbal and written communication ensures the message is understood. Skip the jargon. Clear communication means fewer misunderstandings and ensures everyone is on the same page.

- **Non-Verbal Communication**: Be aware of body language, eye contact, and tone of voice. These nonverbal cues speak volumes and convey more than words. Mastering them helps build rapport and trust with your team.

- **Public Speaking**: Developing public speaking skills through practice and training can enhance confidence and effectiveness in presenting ideas and representing the business. Being a confident speaker is key for everything from pitching to investors to speaking at conferences to leading team meetings.

2. Strategic Thinking

Strategic thinking is about seeing the bigger picture, anticipating future challenges and opportunities, and making informed decisions that align with your long-term goals. It hinges on a deep understanding of your industry's ins and outs and keeping tabs on market trends and the competitive landscape.

To develop strategic thinking skills, consider the following approaches:

- **Continuous Learning**: Staying informed about industry developments, emerging trends, and best practices through reading, attending conferences, and participating in professional networks. The more you know, the better you can adapt to changes in the market.

- **SWOT Analysis**: Regularly sit down and conduct a SWOT (Strengths, Weaknesses, Opportunities, Threats) analysis to determine your business's position, identify areas for improvement, make informed decisions and plan strategically.

- **Scenario Planning**: This involves exploring different scenarios and their potential impact on your business to prepare for future possibilities. This kind of scenario planning helps risk management and ensures your business is ready for unexpected changes.

- **Learning from the Wise**: Seeking advice and insights from seasoned mentors and industry experts can offer you valuable perspectives and enhance your strategic thinking. Their firsthand experiences can help you navigate complex business situations.

3. Decision-Making

Effective decision-making is crucial for successful leadership. It involves evaluating information, weighing options, and making choices that align with your business values and objectives. Good decision-making balances analytical thinking with intuition and ethical considerations.

To level up your decision-making skills, consider the following strategies:

- **Gather Information**: Collecting relevant data and insights from various sources to make informed decisions. The more thorough your research, the more confident your decisions will be.

- **Risk Assessment**: Take a moment to weigh up the potential risks and benefits of different options to make balanced decisions. Understanding the potential consequences of decisions will help you choose the best course of action.

- **Consultation**: Don't hesitate to reach out to your team, advisors, and stakeholders to gain diverse perspectives and make well-rounded decisions. Consulting with others ensures you're making decisions with a well-rounded view.

- **Reflecting on Values**: Take a pause to consider how your decisions align with your business's values and ethical principles, as guided by Islamic teachings. Reflecting on values that resonate with your ethical compass ensures that you're not succeeding but doing so in a way that feels right.

4. Emotional Intelligence

Emotional intelligence (EI) is the ability to understand and manage one's own emotions and those of others. High EI enhances self-awareness, empathy, and interpersonal relationships, making it a vital skill for effective leadership.

To develop emotional intelligence, consider the following approaches:

- **Self-Awareness**: Take time to reflect on your own personal strengths, weaknesses, and emotional responses to different situations. Understanding your emotional triggers helps you manage them effectively.

- **Empathy**: Make an effort to actively listen to others, understand their perspectives, and respond with compassion. Empathy builds strong relationships and fosters a supportive work environment.

- **Self-Regulation**: Work on handling emotions constructively, especially when faced with pressure. Staying composed and avoiding impulsive reactions helps you maintain professionalism and make rational decisions, even in stressful situations.

- **Social Skills**: Focus on strong interpersonal relationships through effective communication, conflict resolution, and teamwork. Building strong social skills enhances collaboration and cultivates a positive work environment.

5. **Adaptability & Resilience**

Adaptability is the ability to adjust to new conditions and embrace change, and resilience is the ability to recover from setbacks and keep going in the face of adversity. Building both these skills helps leaders maintain their focus and motivation, even during challenging times in the fast-paced world of business.

To develop these skills, consider the following strategies:

- **Embrace Change**: Instead of fearing change, see it as an opportunity for growth. Stay open to new ideas and approaches, as they can spark innovation and growth.

- **Flexibility**: Stay flexible in your approach to problems and be willing to change strategies when necessary. Flexibility builds resilience, allowing you to adapt quickly and stay competitive.

- **Positive Mindset**: Focusing on solutions rather than dwelling on problems can enhance resilience. A positive mindset helps you overcome obstacles and stay motivated.

- **Support Systems**: Surround yourself with a strong support system of family, friends, and mentors. Their encouragement and advice will be invaluable during tough times.

Unique Perspectives and Strengths of Muslim Women Leaders

Muslim women entrepreneurs bring unique perspectives and strengths to leadership roles. These qualities, rooted in cultural and religious values, enhance their effectiveness as leaders and contribute to the success of their businesses.

1. Ethical Leadership

Islamic teachings emphasise the importance of ethical conduct in all aspects of life, including business. Muslim women leaders are guided by principles of honesty, integrity, and justice. The Quran states,

> "O you who have believed, be persistently standing firm in justice, witnesses for Allah, even if it be against yourselves or parents and relatives" (Quran 4:135)

This verse highlights the importance of upholding justice and integrity, even in challenging situations.

Ethical leadership builds trust and credibility with employees, customers, and stakeholders, creating a positive and sustainable business environment. Muslim women leaders often go beyond compliance with legal and regulatory standards, striving to ensure that their businesses reflect the highest ethical standards. This commitment to ethical leadership can enhance brand reputation and long-term success, as stakeholders are more likely to engage with businesses that reflect their values of fairness and integrity.

2. Compassion and Empathy

Compassion and empathy are central to Islamic values and essential for effective leadership. Prophet Muhammad (pbuh) said,

> "Show mercy to those on earth, and the One in the heavens will show mercy to you" (Sunan Abu Dawood)

- **Social Skills**: Focus on strong interpersonal relationships through effective communication, conflict resolution, and teamwork. Building strong social skills enhances collaboration and cultivates a positive work environment.

5. **Adaptability & Resilience**

Adaptability is the ability to adjust to new conditions and embrace change, and resilience is the ability to recover from setbacks and keep going in the face of adversity. Building both these skills helps leaders maintain their focus and motivation, even during challenging times in the fast-paced world of business.

To develop these skills, consider the following strategies:

- **Embrace Change**: Instead of fearing change, see it as an opportunity for growth. Stay open to new ideas and approaches, as they can spark innovation and growth.

- **Flexibility**: Stay flexible in your approach to problems and be willing to change strategies when necessary. Flexibility builds resilience, allowing you to adapt quickly and stay competitive.

- **Positive Mindset**: Focusing on solutions rather than dwelling on problems can enhance resilience. A positive mindset helps you overcome obstacles and stay motivated.

- **Support Systems**: Surround yourself with a strong support system of family, friends, and mentors. Their encouragement and advice will be invaluable during tough times.

Unique Perspectives and Strengths of Muslim Women Leaders

Muslim women entrepreneurs bring unique perspectives and strengths to leadership roles. These qualities, rooted in cultural and religious values, enhance their effectiveness as leaders and contribute to the success of their businesses.

1. Ethical Leadership

Islamic teachings emphasise the importance of ethical conduct in all aspects of life, including business. Muslim women leaders are guided by principles of honesty, integrity, and justice. The Quran states,

> "O you who have believed, be persistently standing firm in justice, witnesses for Allah, even if it be against yourselves or parents and relatives" (Quran 4:135)

This verse highlights the importance of upholding justice and integrity, even in challenging situations.

Ethical leadership builds trust and credibility with employees, customers, and stakeholders, creating a positive and sustainable business environment. Muslim women leaders often go beyond compliance with legal and regulatory standards, striving to ensure that their businesses reflect the highest ethical standards. This commitment to ethical leadership can enhance brand reputation and long-term success, as stakeholders are more likely to engage with businesses that reflect their values of fairness and integrity.

2. Compassion and Empathy

Compassion and empathy are central to Islamic values and essential for effective leadership. Prophet Muhammad (pbuh) said,

> "Show mercy to those on earth, and the One in the heavens will show mercy to you" (Sunan Abu Dawood)

This hadith underscores the importance of showing kindness and empathy to others.

Muslim women leaders who demonstrate compassion and empathy can create a supportive and inclusive workplace culture, fostering team loyalty and motivation. By actively listening to their employees' concerns and needs, they can build strong relationships and a cohesive team. Compassionate leadership also involves understanding and addressing employees' challenges and providing support and resources to help them succeed. This approach not only enhances employee satisfaction but also boosts productivity and innovation.

3. Resilience and Perseverance

Many Muslim women entrepreneurs have demonstrated remarkable resilience and perseverance in the face of challenges. These qualities are essential for navigating the ups and downs of entrepreneurship and achieving long-term success. The Quran encourages perseverance, stating,

> "So be patient. Indeed, the promise of Allah is truth"
> (Quran 30:60)

Resilience and perseverance enable leaders to stay focused on their goals, overcome obstacles, and inspire their teams to do the same. Muslim women leaders often draw strength from their faith, which teaches them to remain steadfast and trust Allah's plan. This resilience is evident in their ability to adapt to changing circumstances, learn from setbacks, and strive towards their vision. By modelling perseverance, they inspire their teams to remain committed and resilient in facing challenges, fostering a culture of persistence and determination.

4. Community and Collaboration

Islamic teachings emphasise the importance of community and collaboration. The Quran states,

> "And cooperate in righteousness and piety, but do not cooperate in sin and aggression" (Quran 5:2)

This verse highlights the value of working together for the common good.

Muslim women leaders who prioritise collaboration and teamwork can harness their teams' collective strengths, fostering innovation and achieving shared goals. They often emphasise the importance of collective effort and mutual support, creating an environment where everyone feels valued and empowered to contribute. Collaborative leadership also involves recognising and leveraging the diverse skills and perspectives within the team, leading to more creative and effective solutions. By fostering a sense of community, Muslim women leaders can build strong, cohesive teams that are better equipped to achieve their objectives.

5. Inclusive Leadership

Muslim women leaders often bring a deep understanding of the importance of inclusivity, derived from Islamic teachings that emphasise the dignity and equality of all individuals. The Quran states,

> "O mankind, indeed We have created you from male and female and made you peoples and tribes that you may know one another" (Quran 49:13)

This verse underscores the value of diversity and the importance of building inclusive communities.

Inclusive leadership involves creating a work environment where all employees feel valued and respected, regardless of their background. Muslim women leaders who embrace inclusivity can foster a culture of mutual respect and collaboration, enhancing team cohesion and performance. Promoting diversity and inclusion can also attract a wider range of talent and perspectives, driving innovation and growth.

6. Visionary Leadership

Visionary leadership is characterised by the ability to see beyond the immediate challenges and envision a better future. Muslim women leaders often possess a strong sense of purpose and a clear vision for their businesses, inspired by their faith and values. The Quran states,

> "Indeed, Allah will not change the condition of a people until they change what is in themselves" (Quran 13:11)

This verse highlights the power of vision and personal transformation in driving positive change.

Visionary leaders can inspire and motivate their teams by communicating a compelling vision and demonstrating commitment to their goals. They can also identify emerging opportunities and trends, positioning their businesses for long-term success. By balancing their visionary aspirations with practical strategies, Muslim women leaders can drive meaningful and sustainable growth.

7. Adaptability and Flexibility

In today's rapidly changing business environment, adaptability and flexibility are crucial leadership qualities. Muslim women leaders often demonstrate a high degree of adaptability, drawing on their resilience and problem-solving skills to navigate uncertainty and change. The Quran states,

> "And whoever fears Allah – He will make for him a way out and will provide for him from where he does not expect" (Quran 65:2-3)

This verse encourages trust in Allah's guidance and the ability to find solutions in challenging situations.

Adaptable leaders can respond quickly to changing market conditions, customer needs, and technological advancements, ensuring their businesses remain competitive and relevant. They're also open to new ideas and approaches, fostering a culture of continuous learning and innovation within their teams.

Conclusion

Muslim women entrepreneurs bring unique perspectives and strengths to leadership roles rooted in their cultural and religious values. By embracing ethical leadership, compassion and empathy, resilience and perseverance, community and collaboration, inclusivity, visionary thinking, and adaptability, they can create successful and sustainable businesses. These qualities not only enhance their effectiveness as leaders but also contribute to the overall success and well-being of their teams and communities.

Mentoring and Networking Opportunities

As we've touched upon throughout this book, mentoring and networking are invaluable tools in the entrepreneurial journey that can significantly enhance a woman's ability to succeed in business. These resources provide guidance, support, and connections to help navigate challenges, seize opportunities, and foster growth. For Muslim women entrepreneurs, mentoring and networking can also offer a sense of community and shared understanding that is particularly empowering. This chapter explores the importance of mentoring and networking, practical strategies for building these relationships, and its impact on entrepreneurial success.

The Value of Mentoring

Mentoring is a relationship where an experienced individual (the mentor) provides guidance, support, and advice to a less experienced person (the mentee). This relationship can be incredibly beneficial for Muslim women entrepreneurs, offering both professional and personal development opportunities.

Guidance and Knowledge Sharing

Mentors can provide valuable insights based on their own experiences, helping mentees avoid common pitfalls and make informed decisions. This guidance can cover various aspects of running a business, from strategic planning and financial management to marketing and leadership. The Quran emphasises the importance of seeking knowledge and learning from others:

> "And say, 'My Lord, increase me in knowledge'" (Quran 20:114)

Effective mentoring involves transferring critical business knowledge and skills that can significantly shorten the learning curve for new entrepreneurs. By sharing their own success stories and lessons learned from failures, mentors help mentees navigate the complexities of entrepreneurship. This knowledge exchange can include specific industry insights, effective business practices, and innovative strategies that have proven successful in similar ventures.

Confidence and Encouragement

Having a mentor can boost a mentee's confidence, providing reassurance and encouragement during challenging times. Knowing that someone with experience believes in their potential can be a powerful motivator. Prophet Muhammad (pbuh) said,

> "None of you truly believes until he loves for his brother what he loves for himself" (Sahih Muslim)

This hadith highlights the importance of supporting and uplifting others.

Confidence is crucial for entrepreneurs, who often face numerous challenges and setbacks. A mentor's encouragement can help mentees maintain a positive outlook, build self-esteem, and persist through difficult phases. Mentors can provide constructive feedback, assisting mentees to recognise their strengths and areas for improvement. This supportive relationship fosters a growth mindset, enabling mentees to approach their business ventures with greater assurance and determination.

Networking and Opportunities

Mentors open doors to new opportunities by connecting mentees with their professional networks. This can lead to partnerships, collaborations, and new business ventures. Networking through a mentor's contacts can also provide access to industry insights and resources that might be unavailable.

Networking is critical to business success, offering access to potential clients, investors, and industry leaders. Mentors can facilitate introductions to influential individuals, helping mentees expand their professional circles and gain credibility. Additionally, mentors can guide mentees on how to effectively network, including best practices for building and maintaining professional relationships.

Personal Growth and Development

Mentoring relationships often extend beyond professional guidance to include personal growth and development. Mentors can help mentees develop important soft skills such as communication, resilience, and emotional intelligence. This holistic approach to development is crucial for long-term success in both business and personal life.

Personal growth is an integral part of entrepreneurship, requiring the development of skills that enhance both professional and personal well-being. Mentors can offer insights on work-life balance, stress management, and self-care, ensuring that mentees maintain a healthy and sustainable approach to their business endeavours. Emotional intelligence, in particular, is vital for effective leadership, enabling entrepreneurs to navigate interpersonal relationships with empathy and understanding. Mentors can provide practical advice on cultivating these skills, drawing from their own experiences and expertise.

Long-Term Relationship Building

Mentoring relationships often evolve into long-term partnerships that extend beyond the initial scope of guidance. These enduring relationships can offer continuous support and collaboration, benefiting mentors and mentees. As mentees grow and succeed, they may become mentors, creating a cycle of knowledge sharing and mutual growth.

Long-term mentoring relationships provide a stable support system, fostering a sense of loyalty and commitment between mentor and mentee. This continuity allows for deeper insights and more personalised advice as mentors become more familiar with the mentee's business and personal goals. The ongoing nature of these relationships also provides opportunities for mentors and mentees to collaborate on new projects and initiatives, leveraging each other's strengths and expertise for mutual benefit.

Fostering a Culture of Mentorship

Encouraging a culture of mentorship within the entrepreneurial community can amplify the benefits of individual mentoring relationships. By promoting mentorship as a key component of professional development, businesses and organisations can create environments where knowledge sharing and mutual support are valued and prioritised.

A culture of mentorship can be fostered through formal programs, peer-to-peer mentoring, and networking events that facilitate mentor-mentee connections. Organisations can provide resources and training for mentors to enhance their effectiveness, ensuring that mentees receive high-quality guidance and support. Additionally, recognising and celebrating successful mentoring relationships can inspire others to seek and engage in mentorship, further strengthening the entrepreneurial ecosystem.

Finding and Building Mentoring Relationships

Establishing a successful mentoring relationship involves finding the right mentor, building a strong connection, and maintaining a productive relationship. If you're a Muslim female entrepreneur, here are practical steps to finding the right mentor for you:

Identifying Potential Mentors

Start by identifying individuals with the experience, knowledge, and values that align with your goals. Potential mentors can be found within professional associations, industry events, business networks, or your community. It's important to seek mentors who understand the unique challenges faced by Muslim women entrepreneurs. Look for mentors with a track record of success, have expertise in your industry, and share similar ethical and cultural values.

Consider expanding your search to include online platforms such as LinkedIn, professional forums, and mentorship programs designed explicitly for women entrepreneurs. These platforms can provide access to a broader pool of potential mentors and facilitate connections that might not be available locally.

Reaching Out and Making a Connection

Once you've identified potential mentors, reach out with a clear and respectful request. Explain why you admire their work, how their experience aligns with your goals, and what you hope to gain from the mentoring relationship. Be specific about what you are looking for, whether it's regular meetings, occasional advice, or specific guidance on certain topics.

When reaching out, personalise your message to show that you've done your research and are genuinely interested in their expertise. Highlight specific achievements or projects that inspired you and explain how their guidance can help you overcome your current challenges. Being clear about your expectations and goals can help potential mentors understand how they can best support you.

Building a Strong Relationship

Building a strong mentoring relationship requires effort and commitment from both parties. Here are some tips:

- **Be Respectful and Grateful**: Show appreciation for your mentor's time and advice. Respect their boundaries and be mindful of their schedule. A simple thank you note or acknowledgement of their contributions can go a long way in building goodwill.

- **Be Prepared and Proactive**: Come to meetings with specific questions or topics you want to discuss. Prepare an agenda and outline your key concerns and goals. Take the initiative to implement your mentor's advice and share updates on your progress.

- **Be Open and Honest**: Share your challenges and successes openly. Honest communication is key to a productive mentoring relationship. Don't be afraid to discuss your fears, uncertainties, and failures; these conversations can lead to valuable insights and guidance.

- **Be Patient and Committed**: Building a strong relationship takes time. Be patient and committed to the process, and be willing to invest the time and effort needed. Consistency in your interactions and follow-through on commitments are crucial for developing trust and respect.

Additionally, consider setting clear goals and milestones for the mentoring relationship. Regularly review these goals with your mentor to ensure you are on track and make adjustments as needed. Establishing a structured interaction framework can help you and your mentor stay focused and achieve meaningful outcomes.

Evaluating and Evolving the Relationship

Regularly evaluate the mentoring relationship to ensure it remains productive and beneficial. Be open to feedback and willing to adapt as needed. If the relationship evolves and your needs change, discuss these changes and adjust your relationship accordingly.

Set aside time to reflect on your progress with your mentor. Consider what aspects of the relationship have been most helpful and what areas need improvement. Schedule periodic check-ins with them to discuss your overall experience and any adjustments that might enhance the mentoring process.

If the relationship is no longer meeting your needs, have an open and honest conversation with your mentor about how to move forward. This might involve redefining the scope of the mentorship, seeking additional mentors to address specific areas, or gracefully concluding the formal mentoring relationship while maintaining a professional connection.

Additional Tips for Success

- **Create a Mentorship Agreement**: Draft a mentorship agreement that outlines the expectations, frequency of meetings, confidentiality, and goals of the mentoring relationship. This formalises the arrangement and ensures that both parties are aligned.

- **Celebrate Milestones**: Acknowledge and celebrate significant milestones and achievements. This not only reinforces the progress you've made but also strengthens the mentor-mentee bond.

- **Give Back**: As you benefit from the mentorship, look for ways to give back. This could involve sharing what you've learned with peers, supporting your mentor in their projects, or eventually becoming a mentor yourself.

The Importance of Networking

After exploring the undeniable advantages of mentorship as a Muslim women entrepreneur, we'll discuss the importance of networking.

Networking is building and maintaining relationships with people who can provide support, information, and opportunities. For Muslim women entrepreneurs, effective networking can open doors to new business opportunities, partnerships, and valuable industry insights. Beyond these practical benefits, networking also fosters a sense of community and mutual support, which can be particularly empowering for women navigating the challenges of entrepreneurship.

Expanding Business Opportunities

Networking can help entrepreneurs discover new markets, clients, and partners. By connecting with other business owners, industry leaders, and potential customers, women entrepreneurs can expand their reach and grow their businesses. Networking events, industry conferences, and online platforms like LinkedIn can be valuable resources for making these connections.

In-person networking events, such as trade shows, seminars, and workshops, offer face-to-face opportunities to meet potential clients and partners. These interactions can lead to collaborations, partnerships, and new business deals. Additionally, online networking platforms and social media groups provide a space for continuous engagement, allowing entrepreneurs to connect with a global audience and share their expertise.

Gaining Industry Insights

Networking provides access to industry trends, best practices, and insider knowledge, which are vital for staying competitive. Engaging with others in the industry can help entrepreneurs stay informed about market developments, emerging technologies, and regulatory changes.

Participating in industry-specific groups and forums fosters discussions on challenges, leading to valuable insights and innovative ideas not easily accessible through formal education or training. Webinars, panel discussions, and roundtable meetings can provide in-depth knowledge and perspectives from industry experts.

Building a Support System

A strong professional network can serve as a support system, providing advice, encouragement, and assistance when needed. Fellow entrepreneurs who understand the challenges can offer valuable insights and moral support. The Quran highlights the importance of supporting one another:

> "And cooperate in righteousness and piety, but do not cooperate in sin and aggression" (Quran 5:2)

Mentorship relationships often develop from networking, where experienced entrepreneurs guide and support newcomers. These mentors can provide practical advice, share their own experiences, and help mentees navigate the complexities of running a business. Peer support groups and business associations can also offer a sense of community, where members can share resources, celebrate successes, and collaborate on solutions to common problems.

Enhancing Visibility and Credibility

Active participation in networking can enhance visibility and credibility within one's industry. By attending events, participating in discussions, and contributing to industry publications, entrepreneurs can establish themselves as knowledgeable and trusted professionals.

Speaking at conferences, writing articles for industry journals, and participating in panel discussions are effective ways for professionals to showcase their expertise and build a strong reputation. These activities enhance personal brand and increase the visibility of businesses, attracting potential clients and partners.

Leveraging Digital Networks

In today's digital age, online networking is as crucial as traditional methods. Social media platforms like LinkedIn, Twitter, and Facebook allow entrepreneurs to connect with a broader audience, share their insights, and stay updated with industry news. Online groups and forums dedicated to specific industries or entrepreneurial interests provide a platform for continuous learning and engagement.

Building an online presence through blogs, podcasts, and webinars can expand reach and influence. By sharing valuable content and engaging with their audience, entrepreneurs can establish themselves as thought leaders.

Navigating Cultural and Gender-Specific Challenges

For Muslim women entrepreneurs, networking also involves navigating cultural and gender-specific challenges. Building relationships within culturally sensitive and supportive networks can provide a safe space to discuss unique challenges and find tailored solutions. Organisations and networks focused on supporting women and Muslim entrepreneurs can offer targeted resources, events, and mentorship programs.

Continuous Learning and Professional Development

Networking is not a one-time activity but a continuous process of learning and development. Regularly attending networking events, joining professional associations, and staying active in online communities ensure that they remain connected and informed. Continuous networking helps them adapt to industry changes, discover new opportunities, and maintain a dynamic and resilient business.

Practical Strategies for Effective Networking for Female Muslim Entrepreneurs

As a female Muslim entrepreneur, effective networking involves more than just attending events and exchanging business cards. It requires a strategic approach and a genuine commitment to building and nurturing professional relationships. Here are some practical strategies tailored to your journey:

1. **Setting Clear Goals**: Before engaging in networking activities, take a moment to set clear goals for what you want to achieve. Whether it's finding potential clients, learning about industry trends, or seeking partnerships, having clear objectives will focus your efforts and lead to meaningful connections. Define specific outcomes, such as securing five new business contacts, learning about a new market trend, or finding a mentor. Clear goals will keep you focused and motivated, making your networking efforts more effective.

2. **Being Genuine and Authentic**: Authenticity is key to building lasting relationships. Be genuine in your interactions and show a sincere interest in others. Networking is not just about what you can gain but how you can support and add value to others. Approach conversations with a mindset of giving rather than taking. Offer your help, share your expertise, and listen actively to understand the needs and interests of

others. Authentic relationships are built on trust and mutual respect, essential for long-term success.

3. **Following Up and Staying Connected**: Following up is crucial for maintaining connections. After meeting someone, send a follow-up email or message to express your appreciation and reinforce the connection. Mention something specific from your conversation to show you were attentive and genuinely interested. Stay in touch through regular communication, whether sharing industry news, offering assistance, or simply checking in. Regular follow-ups keep the relationship alive and can lead to new opportunities down the line.

4. **Leveraging Online Platforms**: Online platforms can be powerful tools for networking. LinkedIn, industry forums, and social media groups provide opportunities to connect with professionals worldwide. Create a compelling LinkedIn profile highlighting your skills, experiences, and accomplishments. Participate in online discussions, join relevant groups, and share valuable content to build your online presence and network. Regularly update your profile and engage with your connections by liking, commenting, and sharing their posts.

5. **Participating in Industry Events**: Industry events, conferences, and trade shows are excellent networking opportunities. Attend these events regularly, participate in sessions, and engage with other attendees. Prepare by researching the event, setting goals, and planning your approach. Create an elevator pitch that clearly explains who you are and what you do. Take business cards and be ready to exchange contact information. Follow up with the people you meet after the event to reinforce the connection and explore potential collaborations.

6. **Building a Personal Brand**: Your brand is how you present yourself to the world. It encompasses your values, expertise, and personality. Building a strong personal brand can enhance your networking efforts by making you more recognisable and trustworthy. Share your knowledge through speaking engagements, writing articles, or creating content that showcases your expertise. Consistently professionally

present yourself both online and offline. A strong personal brand helps you stand out and attracts like-minded professionals to your network.

7. **Engaging in Community and Volunteer Work**: Getting involved in community and volunteer work opens up more networking opportunities. Whether you join professional associations, volunteer for industry-related causes, or participate in community events, you'll meet like-minded individuals, fostering meaningful professional connections. Volunteering also demonstrates your commitment to giving back, boosting your reputation within your industry.

8. **Seeking Mentorship and Offering to Mentor**: As discussed, mentorship can be a valuable aspect of networking. Seek out mentors who can provide guidance, support, and insight based on their experiences. Be open to learning and applying their advice to your career. Additionally, consider mentoring those with less experience. Mentoring others not only helps them but also reinforces your own knowledge and skills. This reciprocal relationship fosters mutual growth and expands your professional network.

9. **Practicing Active Listening**: Active listening is a critical skill in effective networking. When engaging with others, prioritise listening over speaking. Show genuine interest in what the other person is saying, ask thoughtful questions, and respond appropriately. Active listening helps you understand the other person's needs and interests, making it easier to find ways to collaborate and support each other.

10. **Attending Workshops**: Continuous learning and professional development are essential for staying current in your field and enhancing your networking efforts. Attend workshops, webinars, and professional development programs to acquire new skills and knowledge. These events offer chances to connect with other professionals who share your commitment to personal and professional growth. Engaging in these activities demonstrates your dedication to self-improvement and can attract like-minded individuals to your network.

Case Studies of Successful Networking and Mentoring

To illustrate the impact of mentoring and networking, let's explore some case studies of successful Muslim women entrepreneurs who have leveraged these resources to achieve remarkable success.

Lubna Olayan: Banking on Mentorship

Lubna Olayan is a prominent Saudi businesswoman and the CEO of Olayan Financing Company. Throughout her career, she has emphasised the importance of mentorship and networking. Lubna credits her success to the guidance and support she received from mentors and her proactive approach to building professional relationships.

From the outset of her career, Lubna sought out mentors who could provide valuable insights and guidance. These mentors helped her navigate the complexities of the business world and offered support during challenging times. Lubna's ability to learn from experienced professionals and apply their advice to her business decisions has been instrumental in her success.

Lubna's networking efforts have allowed her to establish strong connections with global business leaders, opening doors to new opportunities and collaborations. She actively participates in international business forums, industry conferences, and networking events, where she engages with peers and potential partners. These connections have not only enhanced her business ventures but also positioned her as a key player in the global business community.

One notable aspect of Lubna's networking strategy is her focus on building a diverse and inclusive professional network. She understands the value of having a wide range of perspectives and experiences, contributing to her ability to innovate and adapt in a rapidly changing business environment. Her story highlights the value of mentorship and the importance of building a diverse and robust professional network.

Fatima Al Jaber: Engineering Success through Networks

Fatima Al Jaber is an Emirati engineer and businesswoman who has made significant strides in the construction industry. As the Chief Operating Officer of Al Jaber Group, Fatima has leveraged her professional network to drive business growth and innovation.

Fatima's active participation in industry associations and networking events has enhanced her visibility and credibility. She regularly attends international construction and engineering conferences, where she shares her expertise and learns from others. These events allow her to connect with industry peers, government officials, and business leaders.

Through strategic networking, Fatima has built strong relationships that have been instrumental in her success. For instance, her connections with government officials have facilitated the approval of key projects and secured funding for large-scale developments. Additionally, her relationships with other industry leaders have led to valuable collaborations and partnerships, driving innovation and efficiency within her company.

Fatima also places a high value on mentoring and has established mentorship programs within her organisation to support the development of young engineers, particularly women. By sharing her knowledge and experience, she helps the next generation of engineers navigate their careers and achieve their professional goals. Fatima's experience underscores the importance of strategic networking in achieving business objectives and highlights the role of mentoring in fostering industry growth.

Reem Asaad: Advocating through Mentoring

Reem Asaad is a Saudi financial advisor and advocate for women's rights. She is known for her successful campaign to improve working conditions for women in Saudi Arabia's retail sector. Reem's mentorship relationships and networking efforts have played a crucial role in her advocacy work.

Reem began her campaign by leveraging her professional network to raise awareness about the challenges faced by women in the retail sector. She connected with industry leaders, policymakers, and activists who shared her vision for change. Through these connections, she was able to gather support and amplify her message.

Mentorship played a significant role in Reem's journey. Experienced advocates and business leaders provided her with guidance on how to effectively communicate her message and navigate the political landscape. These mentors helped her develop strategies to engage with stakeholders and drive her campaign forward.

Reem's networking efforts extended to building alliances with international organisations and media outlets, which helped bring global attention to her cause. By collaborating with these organisations, she was able to exert pressure on local policymakers and drive legislative changes that improved working conditions for women.

Reem's story demonstrates how mentoring and networking can be powerful tools for advocacy and social entrepreneurship. Her ability to leverage these resources has not only led to significant social impact but also inspired other women to pursue advocacy work and challenge societal norms.

Conclusion

Mentoring and networking are essential components of entrepreneurial success. For Muslim women entrepreneurs, these resources provide valuable guidance, support, and opportunities that can help them navigate the challenges of business and achieve long-term growth.

Chapter Seven

Future Outlook and Call to Action

Harnessing the Potential of Muslim Women in Business

In the dynamic landscape of the global economy, the potential of Muslim women entrepreneurs remains an underutilised asset. As we move forward, it's crucial to harness this potential to foster sustainable economic development and promote gender-inclusive policies and initiatives. This chapter explores the future outlook for Muslim women in business, highlighting the steps needed to unlock their full potential and the benefits this brings to the broader economy and society.

The Current Landscape

Muslim women entrepreneurs are making significant strides in various industries worldwide. From technology and finance to fashion and healthcare, these women are breaking barriers and setting new benchmarks. They're launching innovative startups, leading established businesses, and contributing substantially to their communities and economies. Yet, despite these achievements, many still face substantial challenges, including limited access to capital, cultural and societal constraints, and a lack of mentorship and networking opportunities.

The Quran calls for Muslims to seek knowledge and engage in productive work. It states,

> "And whatever good you do - indeed, Allah is Knowing of it" (Quran 2:197)

This verse underscores the value of contributing to society through work and enterprise. By championing Muslim women entrepreneurs, we're not only upholding this Quranic principle but also promoting economic growth and social progress. Empowering these women can lead to diverse business perspectives, innovative solutions, and a more inclusive economy.

Steps to Harness the Potential

Several strategic steps need to be taken to fully harness Muslim women's potential in business. These include enhancing access to education and training, improving access to financial resources, fostering supportive policies, and promoting an inclusive entrepreneurial ecosystem.

Enhancing Access to Education and Training

As discussed in Chapters 4 and 5, education and training are fundamental to empowering Muslim women entrepreneurs. By providing access to quality education and vocational training, we can equip women with the skills and knowledge needed to succeed in business. Here's how we can make it happen:

- **Formal Education**: Encouraging more women to pursue higher education in entrepreneurship-related fields, such as business administration, finance, and technology. Scholarships and financial aid programs for women can help increase access to higher education. Plus, educational institutions should create inclusive environments that support women and address gender biases.

- **Vocational Training**: Providing accessible vocational training programs is key. This should be done by focusing on practical skills, such as marketing, accounting, and digital literacy, and building programs tailored to the needs of women from diverse backgrounds. Plus, partnering with local businesses will help tailor training to real industry needs.

- **Continuous Learning**: Promoting lifelong learning through online courses, workshops, and seminars will enable women to stay up-to-date with industry trends and continuously improve their skills. Online platforms such as Coursera, Udemy, and LinkedIn Learning offer flexible learning opportunities that fit into the busy schedules of working women and mothers. It's all about keeping up with industry trends and continuously honing skills.

Improving Access to Financial Resources

Access to financial resources is critical for starting and growing a business. However, many Muslim women entrepreneurs face barriers in securing funding. Addressing this issue involves creating more inclusive financial systems and providing alternative financing options.

- **Inclusive Financial Institutions**: Banks and financial institutions need to develop products and services tailored to the needs of women entrepreneurs. This includes offering micro loans, low-interest loans, and grant programs. Financial literacy programs could also help women understand and navigate these financial products.

- **Islamic Finance**: Let's ensure women entrepreneurs know about Islamic finance as an alternative to traditional banking. As mentioned, unlike conventional banking, Islamic finance prohibits interest and emphasises risk-sharing, aligning with the values of many Muslim women. It offers more accessible funding options. By organising awareness campaigns and educational workshops on Islamic financial products, we can help women leverage these resources.

- **Crowdfunding and Peer-to-Peer Lending**: Embracing digital platforms for crowdfunding and peer-to-peer lending can help women raise capital without the stringent requirements of traditional financial institutions. Sharing success stories and case studies of women who've thrived using these platforms can inspire others to explore these options.

Fostering Supportive Policies and Initiatives

Governments and policymakers are pivotal in creating an environment conducive to women entrepreneurs. Here's how they can make a difference:

- **Gender-Inclusive Policies**: Develop workplace policies that promote gender equality, such as equal pay, parental leave, and anti-discrimination laws. These measures level the playing field for women entrepreneurs, ensuring they have the same opportunities as their male counterparts.

- **Business Support Services**: Provide business support services, such as mentorship programs, incubators, and accelerators, specifically designed for women. These services can offer guidance, resources, and networking opportunities. These services can be adapted and implemented to suit local contexts by drawing inspiration from successful models in other countries.

- **Legal and Regulatory Reforms**: Implement legal and regulatory reforms that simplify the process of starting and running a business. This includes streamlining business registration processes and ensuring property and inheritance rights. Regularly reviewing these regulations can help identify and remove barriers that disproportionately affect women.

Promoting an Inclusive Entrepreneurial Ecosystem

Creating an inclusive entrepreneurial ecosystem involves fostering a culture that values diversity and supports women entrepreneurs. It's all about collaboration, bringing together governments, businesses, educational institutions, and civil society organisations to make it happen.

- **Public-Private Partnerships**: Encouraging partnerships between the public and private sectors to support women entrepreneurs can provide women with the necessary funding, resources, and expertise. Joint initiatives can address specific challenges faced by women and create more opportunities for collaboration and growth.

- **Community Engagement**: Involving communities in promoting and supporting women's entrepreneurship. Community leaders and religious scholars can significantly change perceptions and encourage women to pursue business ventures. Community-based programs can raise awareness about the benefits of women's economic participation and challenge traditional gender roles.

- **Media and Advocacy**: Using media and advocacy to highlight the achievements of Muslim women entrepreneurs and raise awareness about the importance of gender equality in business. Amplifying the voices of positive role models and their success stories can inspire and motivate other women. Media campaigns can also address stereotypes and promote a more inclusive narrative around women's capabilities and contributions.

Benefits of Harnessing the Potential

Harnessing the potential of Muslim women in business brings numerous benefits to the economy and society. These benefits include economic growth, job creation, innovation, and social progress. When we support and empower Muslim women entrepreneurs, we unlock many opportunities that can transform communities and drive sustainable development. Let's take a look at the myriad ways Muslim women entrepreneurs can make a difference.

Economic Growth

Women's economic participation significantly contributes to economic growth. Studies have shown that increasing the number of women in the workforce can boost GDP and enhance economic stability. By supporting Muslim women entrepreneurs, we can drive economic growth and development. According to the World Bank, closing gender gaps in employment could significantly increase global GDP. In regions where women are underrepresented in the workforce, empowering female entrepreneurs can lead to substantial economic gains. Moreover, women tend to reinvest a larger portion of their earnings in their families and communities, leading to a multiplier effect that further stimulates economic activity.

Job Creation

Women entrepreneurs are key drivers of job creation. By starting and growing businesses, they create employment opportunities for others, contributing to the overall economic well-being of their communities. This is particularly important in regions with high unemployment rates. For instance, in developing countries, women-owned small and medium-sized enterprises (SMEs) can be crucial in addressing job scarcity. These businesses not only provide jobs but also offer training and skill development opportunities, helping build a more skilled and employable workforce. Additionally, women-owned businesses often promote inclusive hiring practices, providing jobs to other women and marginalised groups and fostering a more diverse and inclusive economy.

Innovation

Diverse perspectives foster innovation. Muslim women entrepreneurs bring unique insights and creativity to the business world, leading to the development of new products, services, and business models.

This innovation can drive competitiveness and economic resilience. Women's unique experiences and perspectives enable them to identify market gaps and develop solutions that cater to a broader range of customers. For example, in the tech industry, women-led startups are creating innovative applications and technologies that address issues such as healthcare, education, and financial inclusion. Encouraging and supporting female entrepreneurs can stimulate innovation that leads to more dynamic and competitive markets.

Social Progress

Economic empowerment of women leads to broader social progress. When financially independent and engaged in business, women have greater control over their lives and can significantly contribute to their families and communities. This can improve health, education, and overall quality of life for everyone. Research shows that women are more likely to invest their income in their children's education and healthcare, which has long-term benefits for society. Additionally, empowered women serve as role models and leaders within their communities, challenging gender norms and advocating for gender equality. This creates a ripple effect, inspiring other women and girls to pursue their ambitions and contribute to social progress.

Enhanced Community Resilience

Empowering Muslim women entrepreneurs also enhances community resilience. Women-owned businesses often focus on sectors crucial for community well-being, such as healthcare, education, and social services. These businesses address immediate needs and build stronger, more resilient communities capable of withstanding economic and social challenges. During times of crisis, such as economic downturns or pandemics, women-led businesses have shown remarkable adaptability and resilience, ensuring the continuity of essential services and support for vulnerable populations.

Cultural Enrichment

Muslim women entrepreneurs contribute to cultural enrichment by bringing diverse cultural perspectives and traditions into the business world. This diversity fosters a richer, more inclusive cultural landscape and promotes greater understanding and appreciation of different cultural practices. Businesses that celebrate and incorporate cultural diversity can attract a wider customer base and build stronger, more loyal customer relationships.

Promoting Gender Equality

Supporting Muslim women entrepreneurs is a critical step toward promoting gender equality. By breaking down barriers and providing equal opportunities for women in business, we challenge traditional gender roles and stereotypes. This shift benefits women and creates a more equitable and just society. Promoting gender equality in entrepreneurship can lead to broader policy changes and social attitudes that support women's rights and empowerment in all areas of life.

Case Studies: Inspiring Muslim Women Entrepreneurs

To illustrate the impact of supporting Muslim women entrepreneurs, we'll explore some inspiring case studies of women who have made significant contributions to their fields. Their stories highlight the diverse ways in which Muslim women are driving change, innovation, and social progress across various industries.

Anisa Haghdadi: Social Entrepreneur and Innovator

Anisa Haghdadi is the founder of Beatfreeks, a creative youth engagement agency based in Birmingham, UK. Beatfreeks provides platforms for young people to express themselves through arts, media, and digital technology. Anisa's work focuses on empowering young people, particularly those from marginalised communities, to develop their skills and pursue their passions.

Anisa's success can be attributed to her innovative approach to social entrepreneurship and her commitment to community engagement. By providing opportunities for young people to showcase their talents and develop their skills, Anisa is making a positive impact on society and promoting social inclusion. Her organisation has not only created a space for artistic expression but also provided employment opportunities and career development for numerous young individuals. Beatfreeks regularly collaborates with educational institutions, businesses, and government bodies to expand its reach and influence, demonstrating how strategic partnerships can enhance social impact.

Khadijah Abdullah: Healthcare Entrepreneur

Khadijah Abdullah is the founder of RISE (Raising Immigrant Survivors' Empowerment), an organisation dedicated to supporting immigrant and refugee women who have experienced domestic violence. Based in the United States, RISE provides healthcare, legal, and educational services to help women rebuild their lives.

Khadijah's work demonstrates the importance of addressing the unique challenges marginalised communities face. Through her organisation, she is providing critical support to vulnerable women and empowering them to achieve independence and self-sufficiency. RISE's holistic approach includes mental health counselling, job training, and language classes, crucial for helping women integrate into their new environments and build sustainable futures. Khadijah's efforts have garnered recognition and support from various sectors, enabling RISE to expand its services and reach more survivors.

Dr Iman Bibars: Advocate for Social Change

Dr Iman Bibars is a prominent social entrepreneur and the regional director of Ashoka Arab World, an organisation that supports social entrepreneurs across the Arab region. Dr Bibars has dedicated her career to promoting social change and empowering women through entrepreneurship.

Dr Bibars' work with Ashoka has helped countless social entrepreneurs develop their initiatives and scale their impact. By providing mentorship, funding, and resources, she fosters a culture of innovation and social responsibility in the Arab world. Her efforts have led to the creation of numerous programs that address issues such as poverty, education, and healthcare. Dr Bibars is also an advocate for policy change, working with governments and international organisations to create an enabling environment for social entrepreneurship. Her leadership and vision have inspired a new generation of social innovators committed to solving some of the region's most pressing challenges.

Mariam Al-Mansouri: Aviation Pioneer

Mariam Al-Mansouri is the first female fighter pilot in the United Arab Emirates Air Force. Her groundbreaking achievement has shattered gender stereotypes and opened doors for women in the military and aviation sectors. Mariam's dedication, discipline, and courage have made her a role model for women across the Arab world.

Mariam's journey to becoming a fighter pilot was fraught with challenges, including cultural barriers and rigorous training requirements. However, her perseverance and determination enabled her to overcome these obstacles and excel in a male-dominated field. Mariam's success has inspired many young women to pursue aviation and other STEM careers, highlighting the importance of representation and breaking down gender barriers.

A Call to Action

As we look to the future, it's essential to recognise the untapped potential of Muslim women entrepreneurs and take actionable steps to support their growth and success. Empowering these women is not just a moral imperative but also a strategic move that can lead to significant economic and social advancements. Here are some key actions that individuals, organisations, and policymakers can take to harness this potential:

Support Women's Education and Training

Investing in educational programs and vocational training is critical to helping women gain the skills and knowledge needed to succeed in business. Encouraging women to pursue higher education and continuous learning opportunities is part of this effort.

Expand Access to Scholarships: Establish more scholarship programs specifically for women pursuing higher education in business, technology, and other relevant fields.

- **Create Vocational Training Centres**: Develop centres that offer practical skills training in areas such as digital literacy, financial management, and marketing. These centres should be easily accessible and affordable.

- **Mentorship Programs**: Pair young women with experienced mentors who can provide guidance, support, and career advice. Mentorship can significantly boost confidence and provide a clearer career path.

Advocate for Inclusive Financial Systems

Promoting financial inclusion means advocating for banking products and services that cater to the needs of women entrepreneurs. Support initiatives offering alternative financing options, such as Islamic finance and crowdfunding.

- **Design Women-Centric Financial Products**: Encourage banks and financial institutions to create loan and credit products tailored specifically for women entrepreneurs, considering their unique challenges and needs.

- **Support Microfinance Initiatives**: Microfinance can be a powerful tool for women starting small businesses. Governments and NGOs can collaborate to expand microfinance programs that provide low-interest loans and financial literacy training.

- **Promote Crowdfunding Platforms**: Utilise digital crowdfunding platforms to help women raise capital. Provide training on how to effectively use these platforms to secure funding for their businesses.

Implement Gender-Inclusive Policies

Creating a more supportive legal environment means working with policymakers to develop and implement policies that promote gender equality in the workplace and support women entrepreneurs. Part of this is advocating for legal and regulatory reforms that make it easier for women to start and run businesses.

- **Gender Equality Laws**: Push for the enactment and enforcement of laws that ensure equal pay, maternity leave, and protection against workplace discrimination.

- **Simplify Business Registration**: Streamline the process for women to register their businesses, making it easier and less time-consuming.

- **Tax Incentives**: Offer tax incentives to businesses that are women-owned or that actively promote gender diversity within their leadership teams.

Foster a Supportive Entrepreneurial Ecosystem

Create an inclusive entrepreneurial ecosystem by fostering public-private partnerships, engaging communities, and amplifying the voices of women entrepreneurs through media and advocacy.

- **Public-Private Partnerships**: Facilitate partnerships between government, private sector, and NGOs to create programs and initiatives that support women entrepreneurs.

- **Community Engagement**: Engage local communities in supporting women entrepreneurs through local business associations and community events.

- **Media Campaigns**: Launch media campaigns that showcase successful women entrepreneurs, their stories, and the impact of their work. This can help reshape public perception and inspire more women to pursue entrepreneurship.

Celebrate and Learn from Success Stories

Let's celebrate the achievements of Muslim women entrepreneurs and learn from their success stories. Use these stories to inspire and motivate other women while also spotlighting the importance of gender equality in business.

- **Award Programs**: Establish award programs that recognise and celebrate the achievements of women entrepreneurs. These awards can highlight role models and set benchmarks for others to follow.

- **Case Studies and Publications**: Develop case studies and publish articles documenting the journeys of successful women entrepreneurs. Share these resources widely to provide learning opportunities for aspiring entrepreneurs.

- **Conferences and Forums**: Organise conferences, webinars, and forums where successful women entrepreneurs can share their experiences, challenges, and strategies. These events can facilitate networking and knowledge exchange.

Conclusion

Harnessing the potential of Muslim women in business is not only a matter of economic necessity but also a means of achieving social justice and equality. By taking strategic steps to support women's education, improve access to financial resources, foster supportive policies, and promote an inclusive entrepreneurial ecosystem, we can unlock the full potential of Muslim women entrepreneurs.

The benefits of this approach are manifold, including economic growth, job creation, innovation, and social progress. As we move forward, it's crucial to recognise Muslim women entrepreneurs' valuable contributions and create an environment that supports their success.

Muslim women entrepreneurs have the potential to drive significant economic and social change. By addressing their challenges and creating supportive environments, we can unlock this potential and foster a more inclusive and prosperous society. Education, financial resources, supportive policies, and an inclusive ecosystem are critical components of this effort. Together, we can ensure that Muslim women have the tools, opportunities, and support they need to succeed and thrive in the entrepreneurial world.

Moreover, empowering Muslim women in business enhances community resilience, cultural enrichment, and gender equality. To fully realise these benefits, it's essential to implement supportive policies, provide access to education and financial resources, and foster an inclusive entrepreneurial ecosystem. Through collective efforts, we can unlock the full potential of Muslim women entrepreneurs and create a more prosperous and equitable world for all.

Empowering the Next Generation of Muslimah Entrepreneurs

In today's rapidly evolving world, the potential of young Muslim women remains a vital yet often underappreciated resource. By inspiring the next generation to pursue careers in business and entrepreneurship, we can unlock a wealth of talent and innovation that can drive economic growth and social progress. Furthermore, sustaining momentum in women's economic empowerment efforts is crucial for ensuring that these gains are achieved and maintained over the long term. This chapter explores how we can inspire young Muslim women to embrace entrepreneurship and sustain the momentum of empowering women economically.

Inspiring Young Women to Pursue Careers in Business and Entrepreneurship

The journey towards economic empowerment for young Muslim women begins with inspiration and education. By creating an environment that nurtures their ambitions and equips them with the necessary skills and knowledge, we can foster a new generation of successful Muslimah entrepreneurs. This process involves multiple strategic initiatives, each designed to encourage, support, and enable young women to explore and thrive in business and entrepreneurship.

Role Models and Mentorship

As discussed in Chapter 6, role models and mentors play a crucial role in inspiring young women entrepreneurs. Seeing successful Muslim women in business and leadership positions can motivate young women to pursue similar paths. These role models provide tangible examples of what is possible, breaking down stereotypes and challenging societal norms.

The Quran emphasises the importance of learning from others:

> "So ask the people of knowledge if you do not know" (Quran 16:43)

Mentorship programs that connect young women with experienced entrepreneurs can provide guidance, support, and valuable insights into the business world.

- **Structured Mentorship Programs**: Establishing structured mentorship programs within schools, universities, and community organisations can pair young women with experienced mentors in their field of interest, facilitating regular meetings and progress tracking.

- **Workshops and Seminars**: Conducting workshops and seminars where successful Muslim women share their stories, challenges, and strategies can demystify the path to success and make it more accessible.

Educational Opportunities

As discussed throughout this book, access to quality education is a fundamental building block for entrepreneurship. Educational institutions are responsible for offering programs that focus on business, finance, and entrepreneurship, tailored to the needs and interests of young women. Scholarships and financial aid specifically for women can help remove financial educational barriers. Vocational training and workshops can also provide practical skills directly applicable to starting and managing a business.

- **Business and Entrepreneurship Curriculum**: Integrating business and entrepreneurship curricula in schools and universities would give young women hands-on learning and real-world applications.

- **Scholarship Programs**: Developing scholarships for women pursuing degrees in business, finance, technology, and other fields relevant to entrepreneurship would alleviate the financial barrier holding many young women back from pursuing their dreams.

- **Internship and Apprenticeship Programs**: Creating internship and apprenticeship opportunities that provide practical experience in the business world would give young women valuable insights and build professional networks.

Encouraging a Growth Mindset

A growth mindset is the belief that abilities and intelligence can be developed through dedication and hard work. Encouraging a growth mindset in young women can help them overcome challenges and persist in the face of setbacks. This mindset fosters resilience and a willingness to learn from failures, which are crucial for entrepreneurs.

Prophet Muhammad (pbuh) said,

> "The strong believer is better and more beloved to Allah than the weak believer, while there is good in both" (Sahih Muslim)

This hadith highlights the importance of strength and perseverance, qualities nurtured by a growth mindset.

- **Workshops on Mindset**: Offering workshops and training sessions on developing a growth mindset could be a game changer for many young women. These workshops could include exercises in resilience, problem-solving, and overcoming failure.

- **Encouraging Innovation**: Creating environments where innovation is encouraged and failure is seen as a learning opportunity rather than a setback. Schools and community centres can set up innovation labs and entrepreneurship clubs where young women can experiment and learn.

Creating Supportive Communities

Creating supportive communities where young women can share their experiences, challenges, and successes is vital for their development. Peer support groups, networking events, and online forums can provide a sense of belonging and mutual encouragement.

These communities can facilitate the exchange of ideas and collaboration, fostering innovation and collective growth and providing women with a robust support system.

- **Online Forums and Social Media Groups**: Developing online forums and social media groups means creating spaces where young women can connect, share experiences, and support each other.

- **Local Networking Events**: Organising local networking events and meetups for young women interested in business and entrepreneurship can provide opportunities for collaboration and learning.

- **Community Centres**: Establishing community centres that offer resources and space for young women to work on their business ideas, receive mentorship, and participate in workshops.

Highlighting Success Stories

Sharing success stories of Muslim women entrepreneurs can inspire and motivate young women to pursue their dreams. These stories can highlight the diverse paths to success and demonstrate that entrepreneurship is a viable and rewarding career option.

By celebrating the achievements of Muslim women, we can challenge stereotypes and promote a positive image of women in business. Media, educational institutions, and community organisations can play a key role in showcasing these success stories.

- **Media Campaigns**: Launching media campaigns featuring stories of successful Muslim women entrepreneurs and using platforms such as television, radio, social media, and print media to reach a wide audience.

- **Success Story Publications**: Publishing books, articles, and online content documenting successful Muslim women's journeys in business. These publications can serve as educational and motivational tools.

- **Awards and Recognition**: Establishing awards and recognition programs that celebrate the achievements of Muslim women entrepreneurs. These awards can highlight role models and provide visibility for their contributions to the business world.

Case Studies: Inspiring Young Muslim Women Entrepreneurs

To illustrate the impact of these strategies, let's explore some case studies of young Muslim women who have successfully pursued careers in business and entrepreneurship.

Ayesha Khanna: Tech Entrepreneur and Innovator

Ayesha Khanna is a Singapore-based tech entrepreneur and the co-founder of ADDO AI, an artificial intelligence advisory firm. Ayesha's passion for technology and innovation has driven her to create solutions that address real-world challenges.

Ayesha's journey highlights the importance of education and continuous learning. With degrees from Harvard and Columbia, she has leveraged her knowledge to build a successful career in tech. Her work inspires young women to pursue careers in STEM fields and demonstrates the potential of combining technology with entrepreneurship.

Ayesha's academic credentials are impressive and reflect her dedication to continuous learning. At Harvard, she studied economics and later pursued a master's degree in operations research at Columbia University. This strong educational foundation has been pivotal in her entrepreneurial journey.

ADDO AI, under Ayesha's leadership, has worked on various projects ranging from smart city solutions to improving healthcare systems using AI. Ayesha's ability to translate complex technological concepts into practical applications has positioned her as a leader in the tech industry. Her efforts have not only contributed to advancements in technology but also inspired a new generation of women to explore tech entrepreneurship.

Beyond her professional achievements, Ayesha is a strong advocate for women in technology. She actively mentors young women, helping them navigate the challenges of the tech world. Through her work,

Ayesha emphasises the importance of resilience, innovation, and the continuous pursuit of knowledge.

Yasmin Belo-Osagie: Empowering Women through Education

Yasmin Belo-Osagie is the co-founder of She Leads Africa, an organisation that supports African women entrepreneurs. Yasmin's vision is to create a community that empowers women through education, mentorship, and networking opportunities.

Yasmin's work emphasises the importance of creating supportive communities and providing access to resources. She Leads Africa offers training programs, funding opportunities, and a platform for women to connect and collaborate. Yasmin's efforts have inspired countless young women to pursue their entrepreneurial dreams and contribute to economic development.

She Leads Africa (SLA) was born out of Yasmin's desire to support and uplift African women entrepreneurs. The organisation provides a range of services, including business development programs, networking events, and access to capital. SLA has quickly become a leading platform for women entrepreneurs in Africa, helping them scale their businesses and gain visibility in the global market.

Yasmin, who holds degrees from Princeton University and Harvard Business School, uses her educational background to inform SLA's programs. She understands the critical role that education plays in empowering women and has ensured that SLA's offerings include comprehensive educational resources. These programs have helped many women acquire the skills and knowledge needed to succeed in business.

One key element of SLA's success is its focus on community. Yasmin has created a vibrant network of women entrepreneurs who support each other and share resources. This sense of community has been instrumental in breaking down barriers and fostering collaboration among women in business.

Amal Al-Agroobi: Filmmaker and Social Entrepreneur

Amal Al-Agroobi is an Emirati filmmaker and social entrepreneur known for her documentaries addressing social issues in the Arab world. Her work combines her passion for storytelling with a commitment to social change.

Amal's journey showcases the power of creativity and innovation in driving social impact. Through her films, she raises awareness about important issues and inspires young women to use their talents to make a difference. Amal's success demonstrates that entrepreneurship, including the creative arts, can take many forms.

Amal's documentaries tackle a range of social issues, from mental health to disability rights. Her film "The Brain That Sings," which explores the impact of music therapy on children with autism, received critical acclaim and brought attention to a largely overlooked issue in the region. Amal's ability to shed light on such topics through compelling storytelling has made her a significant figure in both the film and social sectors.

In addition to her filmmaking, Amal has founded multiple ventures aimed at promoting social change. Her initiatives often focus on creating platforms for underrepresented voices and driving conversations around important social issues. By combining her entrepreneurial spirit with her passion for social justice, Amal has created impactful projects that resonate with audiences and drive change.

Amal's story highlights the role of creativity in entrepreneurship. She has shown that artistic pursuits can be powerful tools for advocacy and change. By using her talents to address social issues, Amal has not only built a successful career but also inspired others to use their creativity for the greater good.

These case studies of Ayesha Khanna, Yasmin Belo-Osagie, and Amal Al-Agroobi illustrate the diverse ways in which young Muslim women can succeed in entrepreneurship. Their stories demonstrate that with the right education, support, and determination, Muslim women can break barriers, drive innovation, and create meaningful impact in their communities and beyond.

Conclusion

Empowering the next generation of Muslimah entrepreneurs is essential for unlocking their potential and driving economic and social progress. By inspiring young women to pursue careers in business and entrepreneurship, we can create a new wave of innovators and leaders who will shape the future.

Sustaining momentum in women's economic empowerment efforts requires ongoing commitment and collaboration. Through policy and legal reforms, financial inclusion, corporate social responsibility, community engagement, and effective monitoring, we can create an environment that supports and values women's contributions.

The success stories of young Muslim women entrepreneurs illustrate the impact of these efforts and provide powerful examples for others to follow. As we move forward, let's continue to support and celebrate the achievements of Muslim women, fostering a culture of empowerment and inclusion that benefits everyone.

Find Out More

Website: www.barakahinbusiness.com

Socials: @barakahinbusiness

If you enjoyed this book, kindly leave a review to help expand our reach so others may benefit also.

www.ingramcontent.com/pod-product-compliance
Lightning Source LLC
Chambersburg PA
CBHW050224100526
44585CB00017BA/1970